"How To Invest" series

101 Investment Decisions Guaranteed to Change Your Financial Future

Paul A. Merriman

with Richard Buck

REGALO
educate – empower

Published by Regalo LLC

ISBN-13: 978-1479315963

ISBN-10: 1479315966

This publication is designed to provide accurate and authoritative information in regard to the subject matter covered. It is sold and otherwise distributed with the understanding that neither the authors nor publisher is engaged in rendering legal, accounting, securities trading or other professional services. If legal advice or other expert assistance is required, the services of a competent professional person should be sought. – *From a Declaration of Principles Jointly Adapted by a Committee of the American Bar Association and a Committee of Publishers and Associations*

To contact Regalo LLC, please email us at info@paulmerriman.com

All profits from the sale of this book – and all books in the "How To Invest" series – are donated to educational non-profit organizations. For more information, visit http://www.www.PaulMerriman.com

Editorial & Marketing: Aysha Griffin
Cover Design: Anne Clark Graphic Design
Formatting: VirtualMargie.com

Acknowledgements

This workbook is written to help the full range of investors – from first-time investors to those planning for early retirement.

This workbook is made up of my views on 101 decision points that can – and often do – add or subtract untold numbers of dollars to the investments we count on to keep us financially fit. Many of these choices can also have a profound effect on our peace of mind.

Some of the subject matter will be familiar from my books. However, many of the topics in these questions are not covered in the books at all, and others get much more detailed treatment here. By breaking this into specific decisions, I hope I've made it easy for you to quickly find and focus on issues that matter to you, while you skip over others that might not apply.

If you have a question that isn't addressed in this workbook, I'll be happy to help you with the answer. Feel free to email me at info@paulmerriman.com.

I also invite you to visit my website for current mutual fund and ETF recommendations, podcasts, articles, events, and other information at paulmerriman.com.

Please note that all profits from the sales of my books are donated to The Merriman Financial Educational Foundation, which is dedicated to providing comprehensive financial education to investors, with information and tools to make informed decisions in their own best interest and successfully implement their retirement savings program.

Paul Merriman

Contents

Introduction

This workbook is written to help a full range of investors, from first-time investors to those planning for early retirement.

The bulk of this workbook is made up of my views on 101 decision points that can – and often do – add or subtract untold numbers of dollars to the investments we count on to keep us financially fit. Many of these choices can also have a profound effect on our peace of mind.

Some of the subject matter will be familiar from my books. However, many of the topics in these questions are not covered in the books at all, and others get much more detailed treatment here. By breaking this up into specific decisions, I hope that I have made it easy for you to quickly find and focus on issues that matter to you, while you skip over others that might not apply.

If you have a question that isn't addressed in this workbook, I'll be happy to help you with the answer. Feel free to email me at pm@paulmerriman.com.

I also invite you to visit and sign up at my website for current mutual fund and ETF recommendations, podcasts and articles at paulmerriman.com.

Please note that all profits from the sales of my books are donated to educational non-profit organizations.

Paul Merriman

101 Investment Decisions
Guaranteed to Change Your Financial Future

Every decision in this book is one you will make or have already made, whether you know it or not. You can make these choices by default, not realizing you're doing it. Or you can make them by design, which is how I recommend you do it.

I believe that every item here has the potential to add at least $1,000 to your wealth. Most can add 10 times that much, and some could add $100,000 or more. Together, they can add up to millions of extra dollars for you and your family over the years.

The choices you make are guaranteed to change your future. The future is unknown, and I can't guarantee the results you'll get from these decisions. But the following brief discussions are all based on lots of history, and I believe that history indicates my recommendations have a high probability of success.

These decisions are designed to help you adopt the very best practices of investing, in easy steps. I have tried to break each item down to the basic elements so it is easy to deal with.

This book is not an essay for you to read and then put away. This is a workbook, and it's only valuable to the extent that you put it to work for you. At the end of each item are four boxes for you to check – or not. The first box will let you indicate whether or not the item applies to you and calls for some sort of action. If you check that box, you should also check one of the next three, indicating the priority you assign to it.

"A" priority means you think that you should put this item near the top of
 your to-do list.
"B" priority means you believe there's strong potential benefit for you, but
 other things are more urgent or have greater immediate potential.
"C" priority means this is not a task that calls for action right away, but
 it's something you want to remember and revisit when you can.

Part 1: **The Basics**

Some of these topics seem extremely basic. You may think they're not worth your time. But remember, I believe that each one is potentially worth at least $1,000.

1. If you have money beyond your immediate needs, will you save it or spend it?

Save vs. spend is the most basic investment decision you can make. But before you dismiss this as not worth your time, think about Starbucks for moment. I have spoken with dozens of young people as they buy drinks at Starbucks or carry them back to where they work. Most of them tell me they are not maxing out their retirement plans because they don't have enough money. Many say they make three Starbucks runs a day, even though free coffee is available at their offices. Many also buy their lunches every day.

A little math would tell them they're spending an unnecessary $50 or more every week. With a relatively simple change in their habits, they could easily add $2,500 a year to their retirement plans. They would probably be astonished to know what that savings could do for them. Invest $2,500 a year at 8 percent, and in 40 years you'd have nearly $650,000 (If you make the right choices in the other decision points in my list, you can probably boost your expected return to 10 percent. That would make the $650,000 worth more than $1 million).

—This applies to me.
☐ Priority A
☐ Priority B
☐ Priority C

Although I don't know you, I am pretty confident that you are regularly spending at least some money that you don't need to spend. Can you change a few habits and beef up your savings?

2. Should you save in tax-deferred accounts or taxable ones?

There are huge tax savings available from IRAs and employer retirement plans such as 401(k) and similar plans. If you put aside $5,000 a year for 40 years in a tax-deferred account, you could easily gain an annual return advantage of one percentage point and save $300,000 in taxes. And this doesn't even include the extra money you could invest every year from the tax deduction you'd get for contributing to a 401(k) or a deductible IRA. That's not all. Your employer might match part of your 401(k) investment; if that were $1,500 a year, after 40 years at 8 percent, you'd have an additional $400,000 in your retirement account.

—This applies to me.
☐ Priority A
☐ Priority B
☐ Priority C

3. Should you save in a Roth account (either 401(k) or IRA) or a traditional account?

This choice is all about whether you pay taxes now or pay taxes later. The conventional wisdom asks you to guess (which is the best anybody can do) whether income tax rates that apply to you will be higher after you retire (in which case the Roth is the right choice) or lower after you retire (in which case the traditional is the better choice). Because we can't know the future of tax laws, this is a tough choice. But there are some things that we can and do know.

We know that contributions made into Roth accounts are not tax-deductible. There's no tax refund that you could spend or save. The effect is that you save more money by using a Roth IRA than a traditional IRA. By paying the tax now on contributions, you gain the advantage of tax-free withdrawals after you retire.

Personally I believe that income tax rates are likely to be far higher in the future; if I'm right, it makes sense to pay taxes at current rates instead of future ones. So I recommend using the Roth IRA or 401(k) if you qualify.

Roth accounts have two other advantages. First, they are not subject to Required Minimum Distributions starting when you're age 70½. Second, you can leave a Roth account to your heirs, who can take tax- free distributions over their own lifetimes. I think this makes the Roth one of the greatest estate-planning tools available.

—This applies to me.
☐ Priority A
☐ Priority B
☐ Priority C

4. Should you start serious investing now, or wait until you have enough money?

From my perspective, this is a no-brainer if there ever was one. Investment results depend on three things: your savings, the rate at which your money grows, and the amount of time your savings can grow.

Time is a huge factor in this equation, one that most people underestimate. If you save $5,000 a year for 40 years and earn 8 percent, you'll eventually have nearly $1.3 million. But think about this: Of that $1.3 million, about $434,000 comes from your first five years of savings; that's about one- third of your total, from only one-eighth of the dollars you saved. If you waited five years to start your savings plan (and thus the total was 35 years instead of 40), you'd end up with only about $862,000 instead of $1.3 million. At a withdrawal rate of 5 percent, 40 years of savings would give you a retirement income of nearly $65,000, while 35 years of savings would cut that figure to $43,000.

—This applies to me.
☐ Priority A
☐ Priority B
☐ Priority C

5. Should you save 5 percent of your income, or 10 percent?

When you're young, setting aside 5 percent of your income for the distant future may hurt, at least a little. Doubling that to 10 percent may seem really painful, when there are so many other demands on your income, everything from establishing your family to paying off student loans to acquiring housing. So this is a decision that, while it's simple, probably isn't easy. However, it's easy to calculate this mathematically. If this week you save $200 instead of $100, eventually you'll have twice as much money (at least from this week's contribution) on which to retire.

You might be surprised how much difference this makes over an investing lifetime. Assuming you are investing for 40 years at 8 percent, we can trace the effect of that extra $100 you could save this week. If you saved only $100, you would have $2,172; if you saved $200, you'd have twice that much, $4,345. Those extra few thousand dollars won't change your life.

But think about what would happen if you saved that extra $100 for 2,000 weeks over the years. The difference: $1.34 million vs. $2.68 million. My recommendation is to establish the habit of saving 10 percent of your income. Think of this as paying yourself first. It may hurt now, but eventually you'll be very glad you did it.

—This applies to me.
☐ Priority A
☐ Priority B
☐ Priority C

6. Should you invest in stocks or invest in bonds?

Actually, I think you should probably do both. When you invest in a company's stock (I don't recommend you do this one company at a time, but thinking about a single company makes this comparison easier), you become an owner. As such, you assume the risks of all the things that could happen to hurt that company, from bad management to bad products to increased competition to huge liability lawsuits. In return, you gain the right to share in whatever success the company may experience. If things go well, you could make a lot of money; if things go poorly, you could lose most or all of your investment.

When you buy that company's bond, you are merely loaning the company money. As long as the company can repay the loan and make the interest payments, you don't have to worry about how the business is doing. In exchange for that lack of angst, you agree to accept a fixed rate of return that's probably much lower than the potential for stock investors.

Over the long term, stocks have outperformed bonds in two of every three years, and the difference is typically five to 10 percentage points a year. These numbers apply when you invest through mutual funds that own bonds by the hundreds and stocks by the hundreds or thousands.

From 1927 through 2011, Treasury bills compounded at 3.6 percent a year; in the same period, U.S. small-cap value stocks compounded at 13.5 percent. On a $10,000 investment held for 30 years, that is the difference between winding up with $28,893 and $446,556. Even a small percentage of equities in a portfolio can have a major impact on what you have to live on in retirement.

—This applies to me.
☐ Priority A
☐ Priority B
☐ Priority C

Those stocks, of course, were vastly more volatile than T-bills, and that's why stocks aren't suitable for short-term investments.

7. Should you own one stock or many stocks?

Here are two facts that seem like opposites, but both are true. The highest expected returns involve owning a single stock like Google, Microsoft or Apple. The lowest expected returns involve owning a single stock like Enron or Washington Mutual. Owning just one stock changes the process from investing to speculating. Most companies first offer their stock to the public when they seem to have bright futures full of promise. Only a few live up to that promise, and many wind up losing money or going out of business. Many people have lost their entire investments when they bought one stock.

—This applies to me.
☐ Priority A
☐ Priority B
☐ Priority C

By contrast, there's never been a case in which a broadly diversified portfolio of stocks has lost everything. Every year I give a talk to high school students. I ask them if they want to invest like millionaires. Without exception, they say they do. Then I point out that millionaires invest in hundreds or thousands of companies, instead of only in a few. The good news is that if you have a few thousand dollars, you can invest like a millionaire through mutual funds. That's my recommendation.

8. Should you buy stocks in one industry that you understand, or diversify across many industries, including those you don't understand?

I have a friend who's been a successful banker his whole career, and most of his money was invested in banking companies. After all, he knew that industry better than most people.

His largest holding by far was the stock of Washington Mutual, a venerable Washington state institution that seemed a bedrock of stability. But within about a decade, Washington Mutual morphed from being a local "friend of the family" (the company's longtime marketing slogan) to the country's largest thrift institution, then to the largest U.S. bank failure of all time.

Despite his extensive knowledge of the industry, my friend didn't see this coming. As a result, he lost the majority of his retirement savings. The upshot for him: The comfortable retirement he had planned will be much more modest, and it will be postponed until he's at least 70. My friend's unfortunate experience illustrates the fact that there's no evidence that investing in a single industry provides a high probability of success. However, investing in many industries has provided a high historical probability of long-term success.

—This applies to me.
☐ Priority A
☐ Priority B
☐ Priority C

9. Should you invest in one asset class or many?

This is a variation of the choice to invest in many stocks and many industries. An asset class is a group of stocks with common characteristics. The best-known example is the Standard & Poor's 500 Index, which represents the 500 largest U.S. stocks, including many well-known companies like General Electric, Citibank and Apple. This familiarity leads some investors to think that 500 stocks is enough diversification, and this asset class may represent most or all of their portfolios.

However, investing isn't quite that simple, and some asset classes, including the S&P 500 Index, can spend many years underperforming other asset classes. In my books and in this workbook, I recommend a number of asset classes, most of which have higher long-term compound returns than the S&P 500 Index.

In the 10 years ended in December 2010, the S&P 500 Index made only 1.4 percent a year, including reinvestment of dividends. In those same 10 years, a portfolio that included the S&P 500 Index and many other asset classes grew at a compound rate of about 7.3 percent.

—This applies to me.
☐ Priority A
☐ Priority B
☐ Priority C

My recommendation won't surprise you: choose many instead of one.

10. Should you invest in one country or many countries?

Many U.S. investors believe the companies headquartered in this country give them everything they need. But I think they're wrong. One of the most important forks in the road for investors is whether or not to invest in international funds.

For more than 15 years, I have recommended having half your equity portfolio in international funds. In the late 1990s when the U.S. market was outperforming everything else, this was not a popular recommendation. But in the following decade, international diversification was a great benefit. Over long periods of time, academic studies have found again and again that adding international stocks reduces the risks of a portfolio, provides currency diversification and increases annual returns by about one percentage point.

—This applies to me.
☐ Priority A
☐ Priority B
☐ Priority C

11. Should you invest your whole portfolio in equity funds or include fixed-income?

To make sure you get this right, I suggest you consult Appendix A, B and H in my book "Financial Fitness Forever". *You will find* **Appendix A** *reprinted at the end of this workbook*. If you are frugal, like many of my readers, check with your local library to see if it's available. Whether you buy the book or check it out from the library, I strongly suggest you read all 77 pages of the appendices as they contain some of the best statistical information I have used to make my own investment decisions and recommended to my clients when I was an advisor. Very young investors should have all their investments in equity funds.

Retirees, on the other hand, need stability in their portfolios more than high growth potential. They typically should have no more than 30 to 60 percent of their investments in equities.

I don't know what your answer should be. But I know it's so important that I've already checked the box below indicating that it applies to you. And I've eliminated your opportunity to choose either a "B" or a "C" for its priority. This decision is an "A," and that's the grade you'll get for making the correct choice here.

—This applies to me.
√   Priority A

12. Should you use a newsletter as your source of investment advice, or not?

I'm going to say probably not, because of the nature of newsletters. In order to keep you interested and make you want to renew your subscription (not to mention recommend the newsletter to other people), a publisher needs to keep giving you new information, new insights, new recommendations. If nothing changes, it's pretty easy for readers to get bored. Yet the truth is that what you really need to know and do doesn't change monthly or quarterly.

My advice is to learn how investing works in your best interest, set up your investments on automatic and then focus on other parts of your life. If you do that, you won't want or need a newsletter nagging at you regularly.

If you are determined to subscribe to financial newsletters anyway, you should be wary of their advice. Most of them don't have to pass any "truth test" or be able to offer any evidence for what they say. Protected by the First Amendment to the U.S. Constitution, these newsletters can claim almost anything. You simply have no way to know if the return they report is real or fake.

That's the bad news. The good news is The Hubert Financial Digest (which itself is a newsletter) tracks the recommendations of almost 200 investment newsletter portfolios and reports on the performance. What a difference to see real results, compared to what newsletters claim in their sales materials.

—This applies to me.
☐ Priority A
☐ Priority B
☐ Priority C

I have seen newsletter promotions that claim great performance, only to find Mark Hulbert reporting that they have negative long-term returns. Some of these newsletters sell for thousands of dollars. If you have that sort of money to spend, I think you should either spend it on the services of a good financial advisor or add that money to your investment pool.

13. If you are going to subscribe to a newsletter despite my advice above, should you follow several and try to sort out the best recommendations from each one?

No, I don't recommend that approach. This puts you in the business of guessing on the future. This is a strategy built on overconfidence and hope. Conceptually, this is hardly different from studying the portfolios of several actively managed mutual funds, then building your own portfolio choosing the recommendations that you like best. If you're convinced that you can do this successfully, why not publish your own newsletter?

If you aren't convinced, and you are determined to try out several newsletters with your money, here's the way to do it: subscribe to two or three and split your money into two or three separate pools, one for each newsletter. Let each newsletter guide one pool, without trying to second-guess them in advance, and keep following each one through at least one complete market cycle. Only then will you be able to start judging them for yourself.

—This applies to me.

☐ Priority A
☐ Priority B
☐ Priority C

Unfortunately, one complete market cycle is only a start. There's no reason to think that a newsletter strategy that does well in one market cycle will surely do well in the next market cycle.

14. Is it a good idea to use leverage to invest in the stock market?

Like many of the answers to important financial decisions, the right answer here is: "It depends." Buying a home with leverage is a great idea if you can make the mortgage payments. But if you lose the income you were counting on to make the payments, you could be in trouble. With a home, you can be fairly certain that at least a lot of the value will still be there when you need to sell it. You are very unlikely to lose everything. When you borrow money to make an investment, the investment could dry up completely in a hurry. Yet the debt you took on will still be there. That's a bad deal.

Federal regulations wisely prohibit using an IRA as collateral for any loan. If you don't put up the IRA as collateral, you are free to borrow money to fund it.

On the other hand, it can make sense to borrow money from your parents in order to get started investing.

—This applies to me.
☐ Priority A
☐ Priority B
☐ Priority C

If you are young and can borrow from your parents to make 401(k) contributions that qualify for a company match, that can be a brilliant business decision. I try to look at each situation on its own merits without following some hard-and-fast rule. But there is one old-fashioned rule that's worth keeping in mind: Don't borrow money that you can't afford to pay back.

15. Should you give money to your kids when they are young to invest in their retirement accounts, or wait until you're sure you won't need the money?

This is a very interesting estate-planning decision, and the answer depends on your priorities and the level of your resources. If you make it possible for your daughter, for instance, to contribute $5,000 a year to an IRA, you shouldn't have to worry about whether she will be in good financial shape when she retires.

If you give your daughter $5,000 a year from age 23 to 32 and she invests it at 10 percent a year, by the time she's 65 that money should be worth nearly $1.4 million. If she continues putting in $5,000 a year starting when she's 33, and if she makes only 8 percent a year on this money, her own contributions should be worth another $700,000 when she's 65. The majority of the total will have come from your $50,000 in gifts, which is testimony to the power of compound interest.

When your daughter had less financial ability but more time, you stepped in to make a huge difference. When she had more financial ability (presumably), you were able to turn this "project" of accumulating retirement savings over to her.

—This applies to me.
☐ Priority A
☐ Priority B
☐ Priority C

Obviously you should do this only if you're reasonably sure you will have enough resources for your own retirement. If you can do this, then I don't think you will have any need to worry about leaving your daughter an inheritance ... and that should free you up to spend more of your own savings.

In my own case, I gave my children money for their IRAs for many years. My only stipulation was that if they cashed out their IRAs before retirement, it was the last money they would ever get from me. So far, this seems to have worked!

16. When interest rates go down, should you refinance your mortgage, or not?

As I am writing this, long-term mortgage rates have hit the lowest levels ever since Freddie Mac began keeping track in 1971. Every case is different, depending on how stable your income is, how badly you need to reduce your monthly payments, how much the refinance itself will cost and whether refinancing will postpone the day when you can make the last payment and throw the proverbial "burn the mortgage" party.

It's easy to find suggested rules of thumb for making this decision. Early in my career, the conventional wisdom was that refinancing made sense when you could reduce the interest rate by two percentage points and planned to be in the house for at least five more years. More recently, that figure has shrunk to one percentage point if you're going to stay in the house.

One way to get a handle on this is to divide your monthly savings by the total cost of the refinance. If it costs $4,000 in fees and points to refinance, and you can save $200 a month, then in theory you will break even in 20 months, and after that you will profit.

—This applies to me.
- ☐ Priority A
- ☐ Priority B
- ☐ Priority C

If you're going to spend your $200 monthly savings on something else, then you have merely converted one type of spending into another, and it's hard to see how you are much better off. However, if you use the $200 savings to add to your retirement savings, you have improved your financial position. And if you put it into a 401(k) or similar plan, you'll get a tax deduction, which will also speed up your payoff. If your company matches your $200, you will have a financial home run.

If you're facing this choice, I suggest you go online to bankrate.com and use their "Will you save by refinancing your mortgage?" calculator.

17. Should you put your kids' or grandkids' college savings in a Coverdell Education Savings Account, or in a 529 plan sponsored by a state?

These are the two most popular vehicles for accumulating money to pay for college education. The 529 model, which is offered in various forms by every state, has some decided advantages over the Coverdell.

The most you can put into a Coverdell account in any year is $2,000, which is not enough to make much of a dent in the tuition of today, let alone the tuition of future years. In addition, many people with relatively high incomes aren't eligible to contribute to a Coverdell account. The Coverdell account, in its favor, may be used to pay for expenses while a child is in kindergarten through 12th grade. Money in a 529 plan is limited to higher education.

However, anyone may contribute to 529 plans, which have lifetime limits of $100,000 to more than $300,000 per child. The big advantage of the 529 is the ability to move large amounts of money into the plan. This gets the money out of a parent's (or grandparent's) estate in case of death without requiring the donor to give up control of the money.

—This applies to me.
☐ Priority A
☐ Priority B
☐ Priority C

You can set up a 529 plan for a child and later designate the money for another if circumstances change. You may withdraw the money you contributed without penalty even if the money is used for non-higher- educational purposes. However, any profits in the account are subject to taxes and penalties if they aren't used for higher education expenses.

For most people, I recommend the 529 instead of the Coverdell.

18. Which state has the best 529 plan?

This depends partly on where you live and partly on what you want. Some states levy income taxes on residents and offer deductions for 529 contributions to their own plans. Some states even allow deductions for contributing to any 529 plan.

However, even a tax deduction can't necessarily turn a bad plan into a good one. Some brokers sell 529 investments on a commission basis, taking 5.75 percent off the top of whatever you put in. I cannot see any justification for that. Some 529 plans charge high expenses and fees, as high as 2 percent a year. I can't see any reason you should pay that either.

Some states, including West Virginia, offer load plans as well as no-load plans. The latter is what you should choose. West Virginia's plan also offers the excellent funds managed by Dimensional Fund Advisors. Many states offer Vanguard's low-cost funds; Nevada has the most Vanguard offerings and packaged Vanguard products, all at very low expenses.

Your best source of comparative information on 529 plans is online at savingforcollege.com. The site rates every state's options for residents and non-residents. If you spend a little time there, you are almost certain to find something that meets your needs.

—This applies to me.
☐   Priority A
☐   Priority B
☐   Priority C

19. Can you determine your risk tolerance by using online tests to find the right balance of stocks and bonds?

Not very well. Getting your risk tolerance right is one of the most important and most difficult decisions you'll make as an investor. It's very likely you won't get it right the first time you try.

We tend to have high risk tolerance when markets are high, just as we leave our raingear behind when the sun is shining. And we have lower risk tolerance when the markets are in decline. This isn't hard to understand intellectually, but it's difficult to deal with emotionally.

I have looked at dozens of online risk-tolerance tests, and I think most of them are terrible. They pose questions that don't get to the heart of the matter, which is our fear when the market is down and has erased a large part of our life savings. Some of the tests seem to presume that we can easily tolerate losing 19 percent of our money, but once we lose 20 percent, we're suddenly spooked. Almost all these tests fail at taking into account the different risk tolerances, especially between members of a couple.

I think the best way to determine your likely reaction to market loss is to get the help of a professional advisor. When I was an investment advisor, I used the Fine-Tuning Your Asset Allocation table, (this can be found on pages 141-142 in "Financial Fitness Forever"). That table shows actual year-by-year losses that investors had to endure in the past for various combinations of equities and fixed income.

The following table is from my book, "First Time Investor," and shows the expected returns and corresponding risks of many combinations of equities and bonds. I suggest you use this table as a start.

Expected returns and risks

Equities	Bonds	Expected Return	One-year expected loss
50%	50%	7% to 9 %	25% to 30%
60%	40%	7.5% to 9.5 %	30% to 35 %
70%	30%	8% to 10%	35% to 40%
80%	20%	8.5 to 10.5%	40% to 45 %
90%	10%	9% to 11%	45% to 50%
100%	0%	9.5% to 11.5%	more than 50%

—This applies to me.
☐ Priority A
☐ Priority B
☐ Priority C

You probably won't find it easy to get an advisor to offer a table like this. Facing the reality of losing money may result in closing your accounts, which can be detrimental to the financial health of an advisor.

20. Should you regard the period from 1970 through 2011 as statistically meaningful enough to know what returns and risks to expect?

It should be more than obvious to you by now that anything can happen in the future, and this 42-year period won't repeat itself. However, I think these years represent plenty of the best of times, the worst of times, and the in-between times.

They include three huge bear markets and several great bull markets. There was stunning short-term pain including a stock market loss of 22.5 percent in just one day in 1987. This period included times of very high (at least for the United States) inflation, some years of very low inflation, and a huge run-up in interest rates followed by a huge decline. There were high energy prices, low energy prices, government control by both major U.S. political parties, the end of the Cold War, two prolonged new wars in the Middle East, terrorist attacks on New York City, high taxes, low taxes and, certainly not least, developments that narrowly averted a sudden meltdown of the world's economic system.

—This applies to me.
☐   Priority A
☐   Priority B
☐   Priority C

I know that the future will not look like the past. But I can't make decisions about my own investments without some confidence of the risk factors I will likely experience. I'm willing to lose money on a short-term basis, because I know that losses are inevitable. But my risk tolerance is relatively low, and I don't want to spend a lot of time worrying. Fortunately, I don't have to, since this 42-year period seems to have plenty of built-in worries! And I have built my own portfolio to limit the losses I will likely experience. I hope you will do the same for yourself.

Part 2: Equity Investing

I have already recommended that you invest in many asset classes instead of just one, or even just a few. In this section, we look at the major kinds of stocks you should and should not own and, how much of the good ones you should own of each.

21. Should you include large-cap U.S. stocks, represented by the Standard & Poor's 500 Index, or not?

Because this asset class is a combination of growth stocks and value stocks (which I'll define shortly), mutual funds that follow this index are referred to as blend funds. The S&P 500 Index represents the highest-quality, most reliable U.S. companies, with an average stock market value of $44 billion, according to Morningstar.com. This index is often regarded as the standard for mutual fund managers and other portfolio managers to beat, and it's regarded as tough competition. In fact, the majority of this asset class is made up of high-quality stocks that carry relatively low risks. I recommend that you include this asset class in your portfolio – but only as a part, not the whole thing.

—This applies to me.
☐ Priority A
☐ Priority B
☐ Priority C

22. How much of your equity portfolio should be in large-cap U.S. stocks via a large-cap blend fund?

I believe 11 percent is the right number. Because the stocks in the S&P 500 Index are familiar and comfortable, they make up far more than 11 percent of the equities in the typical U.S. retirement portfolio. But that represents a missed opportunity because so many other asset classes have much better long-term performance.

—This applies to me.
☐ Priority A
☐ Priority B
☐ Priority C

23. Should you include a large-cap growth stock fund in your portfolio, or not?

I say not. The most common proxy for the U.S. stock market is the Standard & Poor's 500 Index, which is made up of large-cap growth stocks and large-cap value stocks. Over the past 50 years, large-cap growth stocks have given investors a compound return of 8.5 percent, lower than the 9.3 percent return of the S&P 500 Index. I recommend you skip growth- stock funds and invest in a blend (combination of growth and value) like you'll find in the S&P 500.

—This applies to me.
☐ Priority A
☐ Priority B
☐ Priority C

24. Should you include a large-cap value stock fund in your portfolio, or not?

Value stocks are those that, for various reasons, are out of favor with big investors and that might be specific to a company or to its industry, or just a lack of interest by the investing public. Low-tech companies can be well-run and quite profitable yet still have no "cool" factor with most investors. Value companies can be identified by statistical measurements, and they are tracked by indexes and mutual funds. Over the last 50 years, the U.S. large-cap value index has achieved a compound return of 10.4 percent, which is 1.1 percentage points higher than that of the S&P 500 Index. The risk level is about the same, making this an easy asset class for me to recommend.

—This applies to me.
☐ Priority A
☐ Priority B
☐ Priority C

25. How much of your equity portfolio should be in U.S. large-cap value stocks?

I recommend 11 percent. These stocks have higher long-term returns than growth stocks and S&P 500 along with lower volatility – less risk. As an added bonus, they are often in and out of favor at different times than growth stocks, giving some added stability to the portfolio without sacrificing returns.

—This applies to me.
☐ Priority A
☐ Priority B
☐ Priority C

26. Should you include U.S. small-cap stocks (a blend of growth and value) in your portfolio, or not?

As mentioned earlier, the average market capitalization of companies in the S&P 500 Index is $44 billion. According to Morningstar. com, the average market capitalization for companies in the small-cap mutual fund universe is much smaller, about $800 million. As mentioned earlier, the S&P 500 Index compounded at 9.3percent over 50 years; during those same years, an index of U.S. small-company stocks grew at 11.7 percent. On an initial $10,000 investment, the 11.7 percent return added $1.6 million to the returns you would have achieved compared to the S&P 500 Index over 50 years. (That's longer than most people's investment horizon, in most long and short periods, small-cap stocks have significantly outperformed large-cap ones, but the opposite has been true at other times. That makes small-cap stocks an excellent source of diversification.)

—This applies to me.
☐ Priority A
☐ Priority B
☐ Priority C

27. How much of your equity portfolio should be in a blend of U.S. small-cap growth and value stocks?

I recommend 11 percent. Based on many years of market history, I believe this is the right proportion in a broadly diversified portfolio that's designed to seek returns higher than the S&P 500 Index without increasing risk.

—This applies to me.
☐ Priority A
☐ Priority B
☐ Priority C

28. Should you include U.S. small-cap growth stocks in your portfolio, or not?

Over 50 years, an index of U.S. small-cap growth stocks returned 7.6 percent, considerably lower than the 11.7 percent for the small-cap blend index mentioned earlier, and the level of risk was about

—This applies to me.
☐ Priority A
☐ Priority B
☐ Priority C

the same. Small-cap growth companies are worthwhile, but I don't recommend them as a separate holding. If you own a small-cap blend fund, as I recommend, you'll have plenty of small-cap growth stocks.

29. Should you include U.S. small-cap value stocks in your portfolio, or not?

—This applies to me.
☐ Priority A
☐ Priority B
☐ Priority C

There's no question in my mind that the answer to this is yes. Over the same 50 years that the small-cap blend index was earning 11.7 percent, an index of U.S. small-cap value stocks grew at a rate of 14.4 percent. You'll find a similar advantage if you compare these two asset classes all the way back to 1927.

30. How much of your equity portfolio should be in U.S. small-cap stocks?

—This applies to me.
☐ Priority A
☐ Priority B
☐ Priority C

I recommend 12 percent. It's true that this asset class has produced spectacular long-term returns, but stocks in this are risky and can suffer substantial losses during major market declines. A 12 percent stake will let your portfolio taste the sweet times without choking on the bitter times.

31. Should you include the NASDAQ 100 index, primarily made of technology stocks, or not?

The fast-growing companies in this index sometimes provide super returns. But these were the stocks that got so many investors in deep trouble in the 2000-2002 bear market that ended the technology-stock bubble. We don't have records for this index that go back a full 50 years, but we do have the returns starting in 1974.

From 1974 through 2011, the NASDAQ index grew at a rate of 11.0 percent, compared with only 10.3 percent for the S&P 500 Index. However, the technology stocks' risk was much higher. In the 2000-2002 bear market, the average annual loss for the NASDAQ was 30.3

percent, more than twice the 14.6 percent loss of the S&P 500 Index. When you realize that the only way to include the NASDAQ is to own less in small-cap and small-cap value stocks, the occasional lure of technology stocks looks much less tempting. If you own a U.S. large-cap blend fund, as I recommend, you will already own some of the biggest technology stocks.

—This applies to me.
☐ Priority A
☐ Priority B
☐ Priority C

32. Should the equity part of your portfolio own real estate stocks known as real estate investment trusts or REITs, or not?

REITs are professionally managed companies that own commercial real estate such as apartment buildings, parking lots, office buildings, hospitals, movie theaters, hotels and shopping centers. These companies have a long history of producing profits and returning them to investors, with timing that's often quite different from the ups and downs of the stock market. From 1970 through 2011, an index of REITs grew at a rate of 12.4 percent, compared with 11.1 percent for the S&P 500 Index. In 13 of those calendar years, the returns of those two indexes differed by more than 20 percentage points. That meant REITs often added return and, very often, reduced risk. I'm in favor.

—This applies to me.
☐ Priority A
☐ Priority B
☐ Priority C

33. How much of your equity portfolio should be in REITs?

I recommend 5 percent, and only in tax-deferred or tax-free accounts such as IRAs and 401(k) accounts. The reason I don't recommend this for taxable accounts is that REITs are, by law, required to pay most of their income to their shareholders, who then must pay taxes on that income. Worse, dividends from REITs don't qualify for the favorable tax treatment that applies to most other corporate dividends. In a Roth account, you'd never pay taxes on that income. In a traditional 401(k) or IRA, you would not pay taxes until you withdraw the money.

—This applies to me.
☐ Priority A
☐ Priority B
☐ Priority C

34. Should your portfolio own gold or gold funds?

This is certainly a hot topic, and my recommendation will disappoint many people who have seen the price of gold rise dramatically since the turn of the century. But think about the factors that make an asset class a good long-term investment. First, it should have a long-term return higher than that of the Standard & Poor's 500 Index. Second, it should not subject investors to extraordinarily high risks. Judged on those points, gold is unimpressive.

From 1962 to 2011 gold compounded at 7.9 while the S&P 500 compounded at 9.1. In that period, long-term corporate bonds compounded at 7.3 percent and long-term government bonds returned 7.1 percent, both with vastly more safety than gold. You can ignore my recommendation and invest in gold, of course. But that would require you to reduce your commitment to asset classes that have been more productive, for example large-cap value stocks (11.4 percent) and small-cap value stocks (15.3 percent).

—This applies to me.
- ☐ Priority A
- ☐ Priority B
- ☐ Priority C

35. Should your portfolio include a diversified commodities fund, or not?

For the 50 years ending in December 2010, commodities returns were lower than those of gold and lower than bonds and significantly less than all the stock asset classes that I recommend. The academic experts I trust have concluded that the long-term expected return on commodities is about the same as those of Treasury bills, minus expenses. Because most commodity funds have pretty high expenses, this tells me that T-bills provide better inflation protection. But it gets even better. TIPS (Treasury Inflation Protected Securities) have higher returns than T-bills.

—This applies to me.
- ☐ Priority A
- ☐ Priority B
- ☐ Priority C

I recommend that you skip the commodity funds. In a taxable account, T-bills will give you more inflation protection. In a tax-deferred account, use TIPS.

36. Should international large-cap stocks, a blend of growth and value, be part of your portfolio, or not?

I believe they should. Large-cap international blend funds add diversification of asset type, diversification of currency movements, and add more companies to your portfolio. This asset class is typically built very much like the Standard & Poor's 500 Index except that it excludes U.S.-based companies. International large-cap blend stocks have produced long-term returns slightly lower then the S&P 500 Index. But because of changes in relative currency values, the ups and downs of these two asset classes often occur at different times, thus reducing volatility. Historically, adding these stocks has done more to reduce risk than to increase returns. But reducing risks without reducing returns is a very good thing.

—This applies to me.
☐ Priority A
☐ Priority B
☐ Priority C

37. How much of your equity portfolio should be in international large-cap blend funds?

This asset class has not been as productive as other types of international stocks. But it includes some of the highest-quality, least risky companies headquartered outside the United States. I recommend allocating 9 percent of your equity portfolio to these funds.

—This applies to me.
☐ Priority A
☐ Priority B
☐ Priority C

38. Should international large-cap growth stocks be part of your equity portfolio, or not?

This is very similar to the issue of U.S. large-cap growth stocks. From 1975 through 2011, an international growth stock index compounded at 8.5 percent, vs. 10.1 percent for the international large-cap blend index. The growth stock index was more volatile, indicating higher risk and lower return. To be sure, there's merit in owning international large-cap growth stocks. History indicates you can benefit from those stocks with less risk by investing in the large-

—This applies to me.
☐ Priority A
☐ Priority B
☐ Priority C

cap blend index. Therefore, I say no, this does not belong in your portfolio as a separate fund or asset class.

39. Should international large-cap value stocks be part of your equity portfolio, or not?

The answer to this one is a resounding yes. Sometimes it is hard to believe the value that investors can get from owning value stocks. From 1975 through 2011, an index of international large-cap value stocks compounded at 14.7 percent, with less risk than either the large-cap blend or the large-cap growth index.

—This applies to me.
☐ Priority A
☐ Priority B
☐ Priority C

40. How much of your equity portfolio should be in international large-cap value stocks?

It can be tempting to load up on an asset class that has performed very well, and this group of stocks certainly qualifies. However, in every way that I can, I'm recommending prudence and moderation. Therefore, my answer is 9 percent, the same proportion as in each international equity asset class except real estate.

—This applies to me.
☐ Priority A
☐ Priority B
☐ Priority C

41. Should international small-cap stocks be part of your equity portfolio, or not?

Among U.S. companies, small-cap stocks have better long-term performance than large-cap stocks; the same is true of international companies. For that reason, this asset class (a blend of growth and value) should be part of your portfolio. From 1975 through 2010, international small-cap stocks compounded at 15.2 percent, compared with 9.4 percent for international large-cap stocks as measured by the MSCI EAFE Index. The correct answer is yes.

—This applies to me.
☐ Priority A
☐ Priority B
☐ Priority C

42. How much of your equity portfolio should be in international small-cap stocks?

—This applies to me.
- ☐ Priority A
- ☐ Priority B
- ☐ Priority C

I believe 9 percent is the right number.

43. Should your equity portfolio include international small-cap value stocks?

—This applies to me.
- ☐ Priority A
- ☐ Priority B
- ☐ Priority C

We can track this asset class only back to 1982, but that still provides us three decades of evidence. From 1982 through 2011, international small-cap value stocks compounded at 13.8 percent, compared with 11.3 percent for a blend of international small-cap growth and value. To me, the answer is obvious: yes.

44. How much of the equity part of your portfolio should be invested in international small-cap value stocks?

_This applies to me.
- ☐ Priority A
- ☐ Priority B
- ☐ Priority C

You may be getting used to this answer by now: 9 percent. This figure is large enough to make a meaningful difference in capturing favorable returns, while at the same time it is small enough to prevent disappointing returns from derailing the whole portfolio.

45. Should emerging markets stocks be part of your equity portfolio?

Emerging markets are countries that are, as the name implies, potentially on their way to becoming major economic players. They include countries like India, Thailand and Israel. There are lots of risks, but lots of potential. Sometimes, as in the first decade of the 21st century, emerging markets stocks outperform those of the developed countries.

—This applies to me.
- ☐ Priority A
- ☐ Priority B
- ☐ Priority C

Many academic experts believe these stocks will continue to have exceptionally high long-term returns, along with very high volatility.

From 1988 through 2011, the MSCI Emerging Markets Index compounded at 12.5 percent, which was 25 to 80 percent higher than most other asset classes. I'll vote with the academic experts and recommend that you answer yes to this.

46. How much of your equity portfolio should be in emerging markets funds?

These stocks have extraordinary potential, but also extraordinary risks. Again I encourage a moderate approach and recommend 9 percent as the right number.

—This applies to me.
- ☐ Priority A
- ☐ Priority B
- ☐ Priority C

47. Should international real estate companies be part of your equity portfolio, or not?

The data I have on this asset class does not go back far enough to be meaningful. However, I believe this is an asset class that belongs in a well-diversified portfolio. I believe the right answer is yes for tax-sheltered accounts (as discussed in # 24 above).

—This applies to me.
- ☐ Priority A
- ☐ Priority B
- ☐ Priority C

48. How much of your equity portfolio should be in international REITs?

As I mentioned earlier, real estate is a specific industry, and I'm not comfortable having it make up more than 10 percent of the overall equity part of a portfolio. I previously recommended 5 percent for U.S. REITs, and I recommend another 5 percent for international REITs.

—This applies to me.
- ☐ Priority A
- ☐ Priority B
- ☐ Priority C

My equity asset class recommendations:

Putting this all together, these are my recommendations, along with a blank column you can use for your own investment choices:

Asset Class	Recommended %	Your %
U.S. large blend	11%	
U.S. large value	11%	
U.S. small blend	11%	
U.S. small value	12%	
U.S. real estate	5%	
Interational large blend	9%	
Interational large value	9%	
Interational small blend	9%	
Interational small value	9%	
Interational real estate	5%	
Emerging markets	9%	
Total	100%	100%

Part 3: Fixed-Income Investing

Most investment portfolios should include bond funds to reduce the risk of owning stock funds. There are many asset classes that could fit in this category, from pure cash (which is awfully nice to have on hand but isn't really a good long-term investment) to Treasury securities, municipal bonds, corporate bonds and high-yield or "junk" bonds.

Higher-risk fixed-income asset classes such as long-term corporate bonds and junk bonds have higher expected returns. However, they also carry higher levels of risk.

There are many opinions on the best way to allocate the fixed-income part of a retirement portfolio, and some advisors may take issue with my recommendations. Because of that, I want you to understand not only what I recommend but why. Here's a brief summary of the reasoning process that led up to the recommendations in this section.

In the final analysis, investors are paid to take calculated risks. I believe (and there's lots of academic research to back his up) that the most productive way to get paid for taking risks is on the equity side of the portfolio. That's where I want to achieve long-term growth. My preference is to use equity asset classes to take risks and use fixed-income asset classes to reduce risk.

Accordingly, my fixed-income choices, particularly for tax-sheltered portfolios, are obligations of the U.S. government and government agencies.

Treasury obligations have for many years been considered to be the world's standard for reliability. This is the level of security I want in the fixed-income part of my portfolio. I believe it's what you should want, too. If you want or need a bit more return, I suggest you seek it by bumping up your overall allocation to equities instead of by taking higher risks with fixed-income.

Many investors get confused by bonds because they don't have a clear idea of what they want bonds to do for them. If you can grasp the brief discussion in the next few paragraphs, you will be able to understand bond investing better.

As far as I can tell, there are only three basic reasons you might to own bonds. First, they can provide you with regular income. Second, you can buy them at one price and sell them at another, giving you the opportunity to make a profit. Third, they can offset the volatility and risk of owning equities.

Most of discussion in this workbook assumes that the third reason is your choice. But you will be a better bond investor if you understand the other two reasons.

Income. The traditional reason for owning bonds, perhaps the reason your grandfather owned them, was to get regular interest income. If this is your motive, you have to continue owning the bonds. You can't sell them just because their prices have declined – or because you believe their prices are about to decline. One other point is worth noting here: If you own bonds in order to stabilize your overall portfolio, you will receive interest income, but my assumption is that you won't spend it. I assume that you will reinvest the interest and any capital gains. Without the reinvested income, much of the benefit of owning bonds will be lost to your portfolio.

If interest income is your motive for owning bonds, I have recommended some specific bond funds for this purpose in the Vanguard Monthly Income Portfolio in my book "Financial Fitness Forever."

Profit potential. When you buy bonds at low prices and sell them at higher prices, you have a capital gain. Usually, bond prices and interest rates change together in opposite directions. When interest rates are high, bond prices tend to be low. When interest rates are low, bond prices tend to be high. If your motive for buying bonds is to sell them at a profit (and there is nothing wrong with this), I think you'll get higher profits (and at the same time risk larger losses) from buying and selling longer-term bonds than from shorter-term bonds. I'm not recommending you own bonds in order to buy and sell them for profits. But I want you to understand that is one thing that people sometimes expect from bond ownership.

49. What kind of bonds should you own to stabilize my overall portfolio?

I have recommended specific bond funds for this purpose in almost all the model portfolios you'll find in my books "Financial Fitness Forever" and "First Time Investor." I suggest you begin with the bond funds in the Vanguard Conservative and Moderate portfolios. For recommendations see http://paulmerriman.com/pauls-mutual-fund-and-etf-recommendations/

—This applies to me.
- ☐ Priority A
- ☐ Priority B
- ☐ Priority C

50. Should you buy bonds individually or in bond funds?

This could depend on the reason you own bonds. If you want your principal back at a certain time, you can buy individual bonds that mature at that time. You will know exactly how much you'll be repaid, and when. If you own individual bonds, you don't have to pay anybody a fee to manage them.

However, bond funds offer many advantages, and they are the best choice for most investors despite their operating costs. The biggest advantage for most investors is diversification. Bond funds typically specialize in government bonds or corporate bonds; long-term bonds, medium-term bonds or short-term bonds, relatively safe conservative bonds or higher- yielding (and higher risk) bonds.

A bond fund can own securities issued by dozens or even hundreds of corporate and government borrowers, something most individuals could never do on their own. Mutual funds can buy and sell bonds much more efficiently than individual investors. Interest payments can be automatically reinvested or aggregated and paid monthly. Maturing bonds can be automatically replaced with newer bonds to reflect current interest rates.

—This applies to me.
- ☐ Priority A
- ☐ Priority B
- ☐ Priority C

While bond funds are not free, they make it easy to buy and sell in small amounts of money, and many of them have relatively low operating expenses and operate quite efficiently. For most people, I think bond funds are the right choice.

51.   Which is better, a ladder of certificates of deposit, or a bond fund?

The answer here can be confusing, because sometimes one is better and sometimes the other is better. As I am writing this, a laddered portfolio of CDs with maturities of one, three and five years has an average yield of 1.0 percent according to bankrate.com.

A ladder is a technique for CD investors who want to have their cake and eat it too. If you tie your money up for longer, you'll usually get higher interest rates. If you choose short-term CDs instead, you'll have much more liquidity, along with the ability to reinvest at current interest rates.

A ladder is a nifty way to get both of these benefits by investing your money in CDs that mature at different times, and reinvesting at the longest maturity.

Here's one example. Assume that you have $10,000 to invest and you want to earn five-year rates but you don't want to ever have to wait more than one year to get penalty-free access to some of your money.

Start by buying five $2,000 CDs, with maturities of one, two, three, four and five years. When your first CD matures after one year, roll it over into a five-year CD. Now you will be earning the five-year rate on 40 percent of your money. Do the same every year, and by the end of four years all your money will be earning the five-year rates, yet you've never been more than one year away from a penalty-free withdrawal.

As this ladder continues, your overall yield will gradually go up and down with changes in interest rates. That means you don't have to lock in today's relatively low rates for a long time.

Another alternative is to get a mutual fund family to do something like this for you. In my Vanguard Monthly Income Portfolio, I recommend a combination of short and intermediate term investment grade bond funds, as well as GNMA and high yields bond funds. As I write this, the current yield of this portfolio is 3.8 percent, much higher than you can get from CDs. And unlike CDs, these no-load bond funds give investors complete liquidity without any early-withdrawal penalty.

However, there is a down side to these bond funds: If interest rates rise, their principal value will decline. With CDs, your principal is guaranteed.

Therefore the choice here is between your desires for liquidity, safety of principal and yield. If current yield and liquidity are your priorities, choose bond funds. If safety of your principal is paramount, choose a CD ladder.

—This applies to me.
☐ Priority A
☐ Priority B
☐ Priority C

52. Where should you invest emergency funds?

This common question has many possible answers. I think the right answer for you depends on the size of your fund and how often you think you'll dip into it. If this is a fund you expect to tap very infrequently, only in severe emergencies, you can afford to take a bit of risk in order to earn some return. In that case, I think it's worth considering a balanced fund that holds both stocks and bonds. Vanguard Wellesley Income, though it's not an index fund, is one example, with about 40 percent of its assets in stocks.

On the other hand, if you expect to tap your emergency savings more often, perhaps once or twice a year, then you should be more conservative. A short-term bond fund is likely to pay considerably more than a money-market fund with very little extra risk. As I write this, the Vanguard Short-Term Investment Grade Bond Fund has a current yield of about 3 percent. Over the 10 years ending in September 2012, its total return was 4.3 percent. A more conservative choice is Vanguard's Short-Term Treasury Fund, with a current yield of 0.8 percent and a trailing 10-year total return of 4 percent.

—This applies to me.
☐ Priority A
☐ Priority B
☐ Priority C

These ideas apply not just to your emergency money but to any funds that you're holding for relatively short periods for specific purposes such as big payments that are due, upcoming college tuition or a down payment on buying a home.

53. How much money should you have in your emergency fund?

This is truly a trick question. On the one hand, it would be nice to have a nearly infinite supply of cash available to meet any need or desire. On the other hand, excess cash won't be working to grow your wealth, so it's a wasted opportunity. In other words, the answer to this is a tradeoff.

As a practical matter, most people will find it easier to build up cash reserves later in life when they are no longer raising children, setting up households, building careers and struggling to pay off student loans. It's normal to have responsibilities like those, and I don't recommend you make yourself miserable with guilt if you can't set aside a lot of cash.

Many advisors recommend that you have six months of your income in an emergency fund. This is nice in theory, but I sometimes wonder how many of those advisors have that much in their own emergency funds.

I assume that if you have a serious emergency, you will cut back optional spending in every way you can.

I think young people should start with a commitment to saving in their 401(k) or similar retirement plan. Put in at least as much as it takes to get the full company match, if there is one. If you have a serious emergency, you can tap into this money by taking out a loan. Doing so will be expensive, but it is possible.

Once you have done, that I suggest you embark on a regular mechanical savings plan to build up cash equal to a few months of your take-home pay. If you have a real emergency, you probably can cut back on your expenses for a while. And if you have not saddled yourself with short-term debts, you'll probably be able to borrow money to do whatever you must do to handle the emergency.

—This applies to me.
☐   Priority A
☐   Priority B
☐   Priority C

I can't give you a magic number for an amount of savings. Obviously more is better, at least up to a point. Eventually, I hope you can build your savings so that you could cover your most important needs for three or four months without having to sell your long-term investment holdings.

54. Should you invest in taxable bond funds or municipal bond funds?

The right answer for you depends heavily your own situation, including your tax rates and other income, the state in which you live and what various bonds are paying at the time you are making this decision.

The Internet is full of online calculators that let you compare the effective yield of taxable bonds and tax-exempt ones. In general, if you're in a high marginal tax bracket, you may benefit from municipal bonds, especially if you live in a state that has its own income tax.

I have never found a hard-and-fast rule that covers every situation. My best advice is to start with an online calculator, such as this one: https://personal.vanguard.com/us/FundsTaxEquivForYield.

—This applies to me.
☐ Priority A
☐ Priority B
☐ Priority C

If that doesn't give you a clear answer, then consult a CPA or other tax advisor who will know how to apply various interest rates and possibly other variables to your individual situation.

55. Should you invest in high-yield bond funds or high-quality bond funds?

In my recommended monthly income portfolio, I include both. The high-quality bond funds will give you some stability of price and reduced risk of default, while the high-yield issues will give you a higher expected return.

However, as I said in an earlier question, for reducing the risk of an equity portfolio, you should choose high-quality bonds.

At the time of writing this, the current yield (present interest rate) of the Vanguard Intermediate-Term Investment Grade Bond Fund is 3.7% and it's 10 year annualized return through Sept. 30, 2012 was 6.1%. The current yield of the Vanguard High Yield Bond Fund is 6.4% and a 10 year annualized return, through Sept. 2012, of 8.4%. This tells me that large investors aren't willing to pay nearly as much for each dollar of earnings from high-yield bonds as they are for earnings from high-quality bonds. The reason? High-yield bonds run a much higher risk of default.

These two funds' historical total returns aren't that different. In the 10 years ending September 2012, the high-yield fund had a total return of 6.7% a year, while the high-grade fund made 6.2%. The risks of these two funds are dramatically different. During the market trauma of 2008, the high-yield fund lost 23.2% while the high-grade fund lost 7.4 percent.

High-yield bond funds often respond to the market as if they were a cross between a bond fund and a stock fund. The academic research suggests that investors who can tolerate the risk of owning high-yield bonds would be better served to use a more conservative bond fund and increase their commitment to equities.

—This applies to me.
☐ Priority A
☐ Priority B
☐ Priority C

56. Should you invest in international bond funds, or not?

I am a huge believer in international stock funds, based on lots of years of data and many academic studies. But the answer isn't so clear with bond funds. It's true that you will increase your diversification if you buy international bond funds. This may help you reduce the risk of default. However, the reason to own bond funds in the first place, at least in a portfolio that also includes stock funds, is to reduce the volatility or risk of the whole portfolio.

In other words, what you want from your bond funds is increased stability. And here's the rub: Owning international bond funds will boost your portfolio's volatility instead of cutting it. In addition, international bonds have historically paid lower interest rates than U.S. bonds with comparable characteristics and risk profiles.

Some investors like international bond funds as a hedge against a declining U.S. dollar. That makes sense in a bond-only portfolio. But if you have half your equity investments in international funds, as I recommend, you already have plenty of currency diversification. You have no need to obtain more of that diversification, especially at the cost of lower interest and higher volatility. Therefore, my recommendation here is no.

—This applies to me.
☐   Priority A
☐   Priority B
☐   Priority C

57. Should you invest in short-term, intermediate-term or long- term bond funds?

This is another classic case of return vs. risk. Long-term bonds pay higher yields but they are much more volatile than shorter-term bonds. If you are certain that regardless of what happens to interest rates and the economy, you won't need your money before they mature, then long-term bonds might be a suitable investment for you. But very few individuals are in that position.

Precisely because of their volatility, and in spite of their higher yields, I don't recommend long-term bonds for individual investors. My suggested portfolios don't include them. As I have said before, if you want more return and more risk, you are more likely to succeed if you invest more money in equities and stick to shorter-term bonds.

The current yield for the Vanguard Long-Term Treasury Fund, according to *Morningstar,* is 2.6% with a 10 year annualized return of 7.6% (through Sept. 30 2012). The standard deviation is 13.1%. The current yield for the Vanguard Intermediate-Term Treasury is 1.4% and a 10 year annualized return of 5.2%. The standard deviation is 4.4%. The return of the intermediate term treasury is 46% less and the risk is 66% lower.

These numbers show the tradeoff between risk and return. You can get more income by investing in the long-term fund − but your risk more than doubles. If your motive for owning bonds is to control risk, this does not seem a good choice to me. I'd choose the intermediate-term fund, which gives you 62 percent of the return of the long-term fund with less than half the risk. That's smart investing.

My recommended portfolios also include a Vanguard Treasury Protected Securities Fund. The current yield of this fund is 2.3%, its 10 year return is 6.4%, and its standard deviation is 4.8%. For tax-sheltered accounts, this is a particularly good deal.

—This applies to me.
☐   Priority A
☐   Priority B
☐   Priority C

Part 4: Asset Allocation and Risk Control

All the academic research with which I am familiar indicates that by far the biggest determining factor of your long-term returns is the nature of the assets that you put in your portfolio. This is closely tied with the level of risk to which you will be exposed.

Although this section consists of only a few questions, they are extremely important.

58.   Should you build your portfolio to get the highest return within your risk tolerance, or find the lowest-risk way to reach the rate of return that you need?

This is a very basic question, and the answer will determine how you structure your portfolio. Most investors don't make this decision consciously, and thus they are never quite sure what they are trying to accomplish. That makes it very hard for them to know what they should do when things don't turn out the way they hoped.

This looks like a simple choice, and in a sense it is, because there are only two unknown factors. One is the rate of return you need and one is the level of risk you can tolerate. If you know one factor, you can probably determine the other. If you don't know either one, you are adrift. And that is exactly what happens to too many investors.

In talking to thousands of investors over the years, I have come to believe that most people have a very hard time determining the amount of risk they can tolerate. Sitting in an advisor's office during a bull market, it's pretty easy to decide you will be fine if your portfolio goes down by some percentage. But when the market actually drops and everything you see in the media is suggesting calamity is just over the horizon, the loss you were so comfortable with feels very different.

I've also observed that during bull markets, investors are quick to choose high returns; in bear markets those same investors are eager to choose lower-risk options.

I think it's reasonably practical to determine how much investment return you need in order to achieve your goals. It's not nearly so elusive or emotional as dealing with risk. How much money do you have now?

How much are you adding regularly? How much will you need? When will you need it? All those things can be pinned down with at least a general level of accuracy. When you have those numbers, you can determine a rate of return that will be necessary to get you from Point A to Point B.

—This applies to me.
☐ Priority A
☐ Priority B
☐ Priority C

I think you're much more likely to achieve what you want by figuring out the return that you need, then finding a low-risk way to achieve it. That's my suggestion for most investors.

59. If you think you know your risk tolerance, how do you find the highest-return investment allocation that will keep you comfortable?

There is no answer to this question that everybody will agree on, and many people never get it right. However, if you can manage to find the right combination of risk and return, a balance that suits your emotional needs and your financial needs, then you have found the key to successful long-term investing.

But how do you do this? There are many risk-tolerance tests available online, and I have looked at a lot of them. They may help, but I don't think they do the whole job. I've never found any test as powerful as actually looking at historical losses that investors endured in various asset allocations. This data can be found on pages 141-142 in "Financial Fitness Forever," in a table called "Fine-Tuning Your Asset Allocation."

To get the benefit of this, you have to choose an allocation, then scroll through the years and imagine your reaction every year to the gains or losses as if you had no idea what the future would hold. You can look at the gains, but they aren't important here. In an up year, you won't have any trouble accepting the fact that you made money. What's worth your time is thinking about the losses along the way. I once described this process as a "fright simulator."

—This applies to me.
- ☐ Priority A
- ☐ Priority B
- ☐ Priority C

All that is the bad news. But there's good news: Getting through the tough times and the inevitable losses will be easier if you have saved more than you need than if you have barely enough, or too little.

60. When should you change your asset allocation?

In **Appendix A**, I have described 10 approaches to this topic. Some are purely mechanical, like subtracting your age from 100, converting the answer to a percentage and investing that much of your portfolio in equities. That would require a change once a year.

However, that's not very realistic. Your needs and your emotions don't change every time you have a birthday. A better approach in my view is to set aside some time once a year to review your needs, your emotions and your progress toward your goals. You should also do this, of course, after any major event that has prompted you to think newly about your future or that dictates a change in your savings rate, your retirement plans, your sources of income or your present or future needs. For example you lose your job or your spouse loses a job or you inherit money or start a new career.

If you have done a proper job of choosing your asset allocation in the first place, then it's unlikely you'll need to do more than fine-tuning except when you experience major life-changing events.

—This applies to me.
- ☐ Priority A
- ☐ Priority B
- ☐ Priority C

Based on my experience, if you are the sort of person who will do a serious once-a-year review, I'm comfortable in predicting that you're much more likely to be successful than if you make some decisions one time and then forget about them.

Part 5: **Selecting Mutual Funds**

The best way to own securities is through mutual funds. The best funds offer professional management, convenience and record-keeping as well as more diversification than all but the very wealthiest individuals could ever obtain on their own. The best funds do this at relatively low cost.

Choosing the right funds isn't very difficult. But it's also very easy to choose the wrong ones; if you do that you may wind up paying too much money and owning funds that don't do what you really need. In this section, I'll walk you through some of the important decision points.

61.   Should you purchase load funds or no-load funds?

As you probably know, a load is a sales commission that some investors pay so that fund companies will manage their money. You should understand that this load has nothing to do with how the fund is managed. It is not an incentive to the fund manager, because the load goes to the brokerage firm and salesman who persuaded you to choose that particular fund.

The load fund industry justifies this charge by saying it pays brokers and planners for steering investors to the best funds. However, academic studies have shown over and over that people who invest directly in no- load funds, chosen without the help of brokers, get higher returns than investors in load funds.

Imagine for a moment that you invested in two mutual funds with identical portfolios, identical expenses, and identical returns. The only difference between them was that you had to pay a 5 percent sales commission to invest in one of them, while the other had no sales load.

Every penny you invested in the no-load fund would go into your portfolio, and you would get whatever return the manager could achieve. But only 95 cents of each investment dollar would go into the load fund's portfolio. On an initial investment of $10,000, the sales load represents $500 that you would never see again, $500 the manager could not put to work for you.

But, you may wonder, why get so excited about only $500? That's a good question. If $500 were all that this involved, the issue wouldn't qualify for this list of topics. But in the scenario I just described, you lose not only the $500. You also lose all the money that $500 could earn for the rest of your life. If you invested $500 and earned 8 percent a year for 40 years, it would grow to $10,862. That is the cost to you of having somebody choose a fund. That apparently insignificant $500 eventually represents more dollars than you invested in the first place. If you could ignore inflation, it looks like a 108.6 percent load. And what did you get in return besides a sales pitch?

My answer to this question, in case you are still wondering, is that you should choose no-load funds. You don't need a broker or planner to pick funds for you, and you don't need to pay for that service. If you learn what's in my books, "Financial Fitness Forever" and "Live It Up Without Outliving Your Money" and in this workbook, you'll be able to pick funds for yourself, save the sales commission and have all your money working for you instead of letting Wall Street unnecessarily divert some of it.

—This applies to me.
☐   Priority A
☐   Priority B
☐   Priority C

At the beginning of this workbook I said every decision was worth at least $1,000. This particular one is worth much, much more than that to long-term investors. If this is an issue that applies to you, the only priority you should check below is "A."

62. Should you choose funds with high portfolio turnover or low portfolio turnover?

Some active managers believe that frequent trading gives them opportunities to be "nimble" investors, getting in and out of stocks at just the right times. This strategy can be the basis of a compelling sales pitch, but the facts argue against it.

Trading always generates costs, and only sometimes generates profits. Wall Street wants lots of trades, because that generates commissions and fees. It's inevitable that funds with higher turnover have higher costs. Those costs are paid by the shareholders, in the form of lower returns. High-turnover funds may experience periods of greatness, and this adds to the allure of the sales pitch. But in the long run, high trading will almost always produce inferior returns.

In his "The Little Book of Common Sense Investing," John Bogle notes that 100% annual portfolio turnover costs shareholders about 1% a year in returns. Some fund portfolios turn over at a rate three times that!

Turnover costs can include sales commissions in the form of retail markups and the spreads between bid and ask prices (wholesale markups). When a fund manager is trying to sell a large position, he is likely to drive the price down at least temporarily. That is exactly the opposite of what's in the best interests of the fund shareholders. It works the same way, just in the opposite direction, when the manager is trying to accumulate a large position in a stock.

—This applies to me.
☐ Priority A
☐ Priority B
☐ Priority C

My recommendation is low-turnover funds. The best examples of these are index funds.

63. Should you invest in sector funds, or not?

A sector fund invests in securities of a single industry. With the exception of real estate funds, which I have discussed earlier, I see no good reason to choose sector funds. A properly diversified portfolio will give you access to companies in all the important industries. If you were to choose sector funds, you'd probably look for funds in popular industries. Unfortunately, that is about the opposite of what you should do because companies in those industries are likely to be overpriced.

—This applies to me.
☐ Priority A
☐ Priority B
☐ Priority C

One of the most popular sectors in 2006 and early 2007 was financial services. Encouraged by the media and Wall Street's experts, lots of eager investors jumped on board only to watch the financial sector fall apart, almost bringing down the whole economy, in 2007 through 2009. My recommendation: No to sector funds.

64. Should you put all your money in one fund family, or diversify across several?

Here's a case in which you can choose convenience (everything in one place) without adding to your level of risk. If you choose a mutual fund family wisely, you can indeed put all your eggs in one basket. Investments held by mutual funds legally belong to the funds' shareholders and are held in trust by a custodian.

When you choose a mutual fund family, you are not choosing a firm that owns or keeps the underlying assets. You are choosing the firm that manages how those assets are invested.

I'm not saying that all fund families are equal. They are not. Whether you limit your investments to one fund family or choose from several, I recommend that you invest with large fund families that have billions of dollars under management.

—This applies to me.
☐   Priority A
☐   Priority B
☐   Priority C

The only drawback to limiting yourself to a single family is that you may not have access to all the asset classes that are most productive.

65. Should you invest in Fidelity funds, or Vanguard funds?

I don't have anything against Fidelity, which has many fine mutual funds. However, everything I know from personal experience, and what I have learned from the academics, leads me to recommend Vanguard.

Over 15 years ago, I started recommending portfolios of no-load mutual funds for do-it-yourself investors. These portfolios were built to replicate, as closely as possible, the work I was doing for our clients using Dimensional Fund Advisors funds.

Our objective was to create portfolios with the right balance of all the major asset classes that I believe investors should put to work for themselves. At Fidelity, and also at Vanguard, our focus was not on fund managers or marketing materials. Instead, we started by focusing on asset classes. For each recommended asset class, we chose the fund with the most efficient access.

My portfolio recommendations have been independently tracked over the years in *The Hulbert Financial Digest*. For the 10 years ending June 30, 2012, my all-equity Vanguard portfolio compounded at 7.5%, while my comparable Fidelity portfolio grew at 6.0 percent. My 60 percent equity portfolio compounded at 7.6 percent using Vanguard funds and at 6.4% using Fidelity funds. These differences are very significant, and they are easy to explain. Compared with Vanguard, Fidelity funds have higher operating expenses, higher turnover, less diversification, and mostly managed by managers trying to beat the market.

—This applies to me.
☐   Priority A
☐   Priority B
☐   Priority C

By the way, I can't pass up the opportunity to point out the beneficial results of the diversification I recommend. In the same 10-year period, the Standard & Poor's 500 Index grew at only 2.6 percent per year while it subjected investors to far greater risk than they faced in my recommended portfolios. Choose Vanguard.

66. Whether you use Fidelity funds or Vanguard funds, should you choose the convenience of using their total-market-index funds, or not?

Total-market-index funds certainly can make a simple portfolio. But how much are you willing to pay for that simplicity? I can't tell you just how much it will cost, but I'm pretty sure it cost you a lot. In both Vanguard and Fidelity, total-stock-market funds are heavily weighted to large-cap growth companies, reflecting where the bulk of all capital is invested. Although these funds include some small-cap stocks and some value stocks, the fact is that huge companies like General Electric and Google dominate the portfolios of these funds – and therefore their performance – just because of their size.

Some advisors recommend using these funds instead of having separate accounts in value funds and small-cap funds. At Fidelity, the U.S. and international total-stock-market funds produced an average compound return of 4.7 percent in the 10 years ending September 1012. The two comparable Vanguard funds had an average compound return of 5.4 percent. For the sake of comparison, the individual U.S. and international, funds that I recommend compounded at 7.3 percent.

—This applies to me.
☐   Priority A
☐   Priority B
☐   Priority C

I don't believe that the differences will always be that big. But for more than a decade I have believed that broad diversification will produce an advantage of one to two percentage points in annual return. And I still believe it. I don't think investors get that advantage in total-market funds.

67. Should you add a concentrated "focus" fund to your portfolio hoping for higher returns, or not?

You probably already know my answer to this. So-called focus funds rely heavily on managers to choose the right stocks and to know when to buy and sell them for maximum results. It's a wonderful idea, except for one little detail: It works only some of the time, and never for very long. Whoever is this decade's great guru may look like a goat after a few years.

Focus funds are like sector funds in some ways, concentrating their assets narrowly in 20 to 50 stocks. This is just the opposite of the broad diversification that I recommend, backed up by the academics on University Street. One of the most famous focus funds, constantly celebrated in the financial media, of recent times was Legg Mason Value Trust, which had a manager (Bill Miller) known for beating the S&P 500 Index for 15 years in a row.

As smart as he was, Bill Miller inevitably ran into the wall of reality, and his fund suddenly became one of the worst performers. In my view, focus funds subject investors to extraordinarily high levels of risk without delivering a premium reward. Just say no.

—This applies to me.
☐ Priority A
☐ Priority B
☐ Priority C

68. Should you try to beat the market by finding the best actively managed funds, or accept the returns of the market by investing in index fund?

This is a tough choice for many investors, because hope springs eternal that they'll find the manager who will eat everybody else's lunch. It's true that there are always actively managed funds that outperform their benchmark indexes. And it's very easy to identify those funds – after the fact. But neither I nor the academics nor even Morningstar has found a way to identify those managers in advance – the only time that information is truly useful to you as an investor.

Morningstar rates mutual funds on a scale of one to five stars. High-scoring mutual funds use those ratings in their advertising, hoping to attract money from investors who believe the implied (but never overtly stated) implication that four-star and five-star funds are a better place for your money than those with fewer stars.

The trouble is, studies have consistently shown that mutual funds rated with four and five stars do no better in the future than those with lower ratings. In fact, some studies show that the four-star and five-star funds actually underperform fund averages after they receive those ratings.

—This applies to me.
☐ Priority A
☐ Priority B
☐ Priority C

Most of the actively managed funds that outperform the Standard & Poor's 500 Index do so because they hold more mid-cap, small-cap and value companies. If you follow my recommendations for choosing asset classes, you'll get plenty of exposure to those asset classes without the high risks and expenses of active management.

69. If you're buying a load fund, contrary to my advice, what class of shares should you buy?

Investors who buy load funds usually do so because they want to rely on the recommendations of salespeople. Those salespeople are likely to recommend not only a mutual fund but a share class as well.

Be careful. The salesperson may not fully describe your choices, hoping to put you in the class that maximizes their commission. It's your money, and you can choose what's in your best interest. (An old saying from your grandmother's days may apply here: "Until you buy, you are the boss. After you buy, they are the boss.")

There are three load share classes that you should understand.

A shares charge an up-front load that is easy to identify. In a $10,000 initial investment into a fund with a 5 percent load, the charge is $500. That money is divided between the salesperson and the brokerage firm with which you dealt. The other $9,500 is invested in the fund. At the end of your first day owning the fund, your account will be worth $9,500.

B shares appear to have no load. Your full $10,000 investment goes into the fund, and that's what your account is worth at the end of the first day you own it. But the brokerage and the salesperson still get paid, and the fund collects that payment from you in tiny increments every day you own the fund, in the form of higher expenses, including a marketing (12- b1) fee. These extra expenses erode your return, and for relatively large investments they cost you considerably more in the long run than the up-front fees of A shares. To make sure that you pay enough to cover the sales commission, fund families impose high redemption fees. This fee gradually drops as you hold the shares longer, then usually disappears after six or seven years. At that time, the expense ratio drops to the same level of A shares for the fund.

C shares charge fees that are sometimes called "level loads" because they add an additional expense (often 1 percent on an annual basis) that doesn't ever stop. As a tradeoff, the redemption fee goes away after you have owned the shares for one year.

If you're investing more than $100,000 in a load fund, you'll almost always do better with A shares if you leave your money in for enough years. You'll pay a very big chunk of money to have somebody choose a fund for you. But you won't be saddled with a redemption penalty or extraordinary ongoing expenses. The percentage load on A shares declines as your investments reach certain minimums.

—This applies to me.
☐   Priority A
☐   Priority B
☐   Priority C

If you anticipate that you will take your money out of the fund after a few years, I recommend C shares because their redemption fee typically disappears after a year. As for B shares, I can't think of any reason to recommend them.

70. How many years of returns should you use to evaluate a mutual fund's performance?

The answer is relatively easy when you're evaluating an index fund or an asset class: Use the longest possible period for which you have data.

(If you're trying to evaluate an actively managed fund, it gets trickier. If a fund has a new manager, do you judge only the performance under the new manager? Do you assume that whatever the previous manager did will continue? If the manager of the fund is allowed to invest in virtually anything, then you have virtually no good way to judge the future. If the manager is restricted to a certain asset class, then you can look to the asset class itself for guidance.)

If you think 10 years is sufficient, what do you do about the dismal (by historical standards) performance of the Standard & Poor's 500 Index in the 10 years ending in 2009? That index lost almost one percent a year. To make matters worse, if you include inflation the annualized loss was 3.4 percent. Is this the result of some permanent change? Or is it just a temporary blip? The answers to those questions are elusive at best.

If you have many decades of data, I believe that is much more reliable than a few years. Looking at the S&P 500 Index, the severe bear markets of 1973-1974, 2000-2002 and 2007-2009 were very similar. On an inflation-adjusted basis, the legendary decline of 1929-1932 was similar to that of 1969-1974.

Long-term returns of this asset class have been amazingly consistent. The return of the index from 1927 through 2010 is virtually the same as the return over the past 40 years.

—This applies to me.
☐   Priority A
☐   Priority B
☐   Priority C

71. Should you invest in a no-load mutual fund, or an exchange traded fund (ETF)?

Actually you may want to do both. I have been recommending both these investment vehicles for many years and have found them to have similar returns. In some periods, low-cost ETFs do better than comparable mutual funds; at other times, mutual funds come out ahead.

ETFs are similar in many ways to mutual funds. They allow thousands of investors to pool their money in an efficient way. But there are important differences, too.

Mutual funds are priced and traded only at the end of each business day. Except for load funds, buyers and sellers pay the same price, which is calculated as the net asset value (NAV) of the fund's portfolio. ETFs, on the other hand, trade like stocks throughout each business day, and their price at any moment may be more or less than their NAV. Buyers and sellers usually pay commissions on ETFs, though some brokerages make them available on a commission-free basis. As is the case with stocks, there is normally a spread between the bid price and the ask price, and this can drive up investors' trading costs.

ETFs are most efficient when they represent asset classes that are very liquid, like the stocks in the Standard & Poor's 500 Index. In less liquid asset classes, such as international small-cap stocks, ETFs are more likely to underperform comparable mutual funds.

ETFs' higher trading costs are offset to some extent by their much lower operating costs. ETFs also are more tax efficient than mutual funds. Of particular interest to young investors and others without lots of money to invest, ETFs do not impose account minimums.

This makes it possible to put together a thoroughly diversified portfolio for much less money than it would take at Vanguard or other fund families.

The best ETFs are those that follow indexes. Actively managed ETFs lose a lot of their advantages because of higher fees and higher portfolio turnover.

—This applies to me.
☐ Priority A
☐ Priority B
☐ Priority C

Part 6: **Selecting an Advisor**

One of the smartest moves that most investors can make is hiring a professional advisor. Even if you don't want somebody to manage your money, you can still derive a lot of value from the guidance, wisdom, hand-holding and discipline an advisor can provide.

I've touched on this subject in all of my books. For more information about these books go to paulmerriman.com

In this section, I'll address a few specific parts of this topic.

72. Should you choose an advisor who is paid by commissions or one paid only by fees?

In my book "Get Smart Or Get Screwed", I made a list of 50 reasons I don't trust the advice of brokers, planners or investment advisors who are motivated by sales commissions. Commission-based advisors may have your best interests at heart, and they may know enough and care enough to give you the best recommendations. But they have to feed their families and feed their bosses' families as well.

Most people who have bought an automobile understand the dynamics at work when we deal with a car salesperson. We usually have a pretty good idea of what we want and what we don't want. We don't need to rely on this person to be a transportation consultant, and we know this salesperson is motivated to sell us whatever we are willing to buy. Knowing all this, we can take this person's advice with a grain or two of salt.

But when it comes to investing money, we often neglect to think about the fact that a similar tug of war is going on. Here are a few of the reasons I don't trust the investment advice of people who are paid on commission:

a. Commissions create a short-term reward for recommending long-term solutions. I think it's better for both the client and the advisor to have a long-term commitment. Once the commission is paid, some advisors may conclude that their work is done. For you, the key to success is setting up a long-term strategy with a high probability of success. Keeping you on track may require a lot of education and counseling. But that doesn't do anything financially for the commissioned salesperson. For the salesperson, the key to success is making new sales, most likely from new clients. Unless you are likely to invest more money, the salesperson is paid to spend time with other people, not you.

b. Commission-based advisors are always under pressure to create income right away. A major brokerage firm recently terminated its 300 lowest producers. What message do you think this gave them and their colleagues who survived the cuts? Do you think this encouraged them to spend time educating their previous investors to make sure they stayed in the game through hard times? Hardly! And do you think those brokers spent much time focused on finding low-cost, low-commission products for their customers? I doubt it!

c.   Commission-based advisors tend to recommend funds with sales loads, higher expenses, and more internal portfolio turnover. That means they are in effect choosing funds that are likely to leave customers with higher tax bills and lower real long-term returns.

d   Commission-based advisors do not have access to all funds, so they can't necessarily sell the very best. Fee-only advisors can sell almost all funds, including load funds they can sell on a no-load basis. I think the best no-load funds in the industry are those managed by Dimensional Fund Advisors; those funds are not available through commission-based advisors.

e. Most commission-based advisors do not have a legal fiduciary duty to disclose all conflicts of interest and to find the best solutions for clients. This may seem like an arcane, obscure point, but it can make a huge difference to the long-term performance of their clients.

f. Commission-based advisors often put their clients into mutual funds and annuity products that impose significant redemption fees, sometimes making it prohibitively expensive for an investor to terminate the relationship with the advisor and re-invest with somebody else, or in more suitable investment vehicles. Clients can feel trapped for many years while they continue to pay unnecessarily high fees.

—This applies to me.
☐ Priority A
☐ Priority B
☐ Priority C

g. Believe it or not, some parts of the developed world have concluded that commission-based brokers are not in the best interest of throe clients. In the U.K. and Australia, as of January 1, 2013, commission-based brokers no longer exist, leaving only hourly or fee-based advisors.

73. Should you hire an old, established advisor or one who's relatively new to the business?

This depends on what type of firm the advisor works for. If you're dealing with a small firm, or one in which the advisor works independently, then I think it's safer to work with one who has lots of experience, including hand-on knowledge of the actual risks involved in various products. If you're working with a firm that limits the choices an advisor can recommend and makes sure every recommendation is evaluated by a second pair of eyes before it is implemented, then I think you can be much more comfortable working with a relatively young advisor.

I personally have an advisor who is 34, a CFP withe over 10 years of experience, and he's likely to be actively engaged in the business for the rest of my lifetime – and still available to help my heirs. An advisor closer to my own age might decide to retire before I was ready to give up the relationship.

—This applies to me.
☐ Priority A
☐ Priority B
☐ Priority C

Because age can make a difference, here's another rule of thumb you might consider: If you're relatively young (say in your 20s or 30s), look for a seasoned advisor with enough experience to protect you from getting too aggressive or too overconfident – or too nervous.

When you're older (say in your 60s), find someone younger who is likely to be available for as long as you and your family can use his or her help.

74. Should you choose an advisor who has a fiduciary responsibility to you?

My answer is a resounding YES!

An advisor with fiduciary responsibility is legally required to act in your best interests and to disclose any and all conflicts of interest. This is what you want and need. All registered investment advisors must adhere to this requirement, which can be onerous.

Alternatively, you can hire somebody, typically a broker or insurance salesperson, who is governed by a less-strict requirement, that of recommending things that are "suitable" for your situation. This sounds good, but there's a big difference.

This is so important that I hope you will take a moment to make sure you understand it. Imagine for a moment that you are my financial advisor. If you have fiduciary responsibility, you are required by law to determine what I need and to find the best solution for me (understanding, of course, that investment results cannot be reliably predicted, much less guaranteed). In this case, you must do what's right for me, regardless of how much or how little money you make for doing it.

But if you are my advisor and have only a "suitability" responsibility, all you're required to do is avoid putting me into investments that are likely to be harmful to me. As long as you do that, you can find ways to make more money for yourself, for example by recommending load funds that will pay you a high commission, even if this isn't the best solution for me.

If you were ill and went to a doctor for help, would you rather go to somebody who was required to find the best treatment or medicine for you, or somebody whose obligation could be satisfied by selling you an expensive sugar pill that cost the doctor almost nothing? This is a harsh way to describe this difference, but if your financial health is as important as your physical health, you should choose an advisor who is required to put your interests first.

Despite its importance to you, the brokerage industry isn't particularly anxious for you to understand this distinction. In a recent survey of 4,200 investors who were clients of brokerage firms, J.S. Power and Associates found 85 percent of them either had never heard of the fiduciary/suitability distinction or didn't understand it.

Your interests are served best when you own mutual funds with low costs, low turnover and high tax efficiency. Most brokers understand this, but they will often earn more money (and in some cases avoid losing their jobs) by persuading their clients to buy funds with high commissions and high expenses, often with low tax efficiency and high turnover. That's a big reason why so many brokerage clients wind up owning what I consider the wrong investment products.

—This applies to me.
☐ Priority A
☐ Priority B
☐ Priority C

When all they must do is meet the suitability requirement, brokers can find it easy to look the other way. As John Bogle once said: "It's amazing how difficult it is for a man to understand something if he's paid a small fortune to not understand it."

75. What education and professional designations should you require in your financial advisor?

I recommend you find someone who has earned the designation of Certified Financial Planner, or CFP. This is not a guarantee of competence, but anyone who has this designation has demonstrated as good grasp of investing and finance.

If you decide to become a CFP, you will have to pass five rigorous tests that cover tax planning, insurance, retirement planning, estate planning and investments. Once you have passed those tests, you'll have to take another comprehensive exam that lasts 10 hours, and you'll do so knowing that the failure rate is about 50 percent for those who take it the first time. When you've passed those hurdles, you must work with a financial firm for three years under the supervision of more experienced professionals.

In addition, as a CFP you will be required to earn continuing education credits every two years and agree to be bound by a serious code of ethics.

—This applies to me.
☐   Priority A
☐   Priority B
☐   Priority C

Certified Public Accountants can earn a similar designation called a Personal Finance Specialist, or PFS.

If I were looking for an advisor, I would want somebody who has completed the work to become either a CFP or a PFS. This knowledge isn't a guarantee of competence. But anybody who's a CFP or PFS has been exposed to many of the teachings of the academics on University Street. And those teachings are likely to result in better advice.

76. If you are working with a broker, will you leave the relationship and do things yourself, or will you make sure your advisor does what you want and works in your best interests?

Lots of investors already have relationships with brokers they like and trust. A big fork in the road can be keeping the status quo, or leaving to do things on your own. I'm not going to advocate one choice or the other here, because you will undoubtedly decide on the basis of the relationship you have with the broker and how strongly you feel about improving your portfolio.

If you decide to terminate the relationship, I suggest you move your money to either a registered investment advisory firm or buy Vanguard index funds.

If you keep your relationship with your broker, you should make sure the broker knows that you're aware of the basic teachings of University Street: low costs, low turnover, massive diversification through index funds, and careful risk control. You can ask your broker how your investments stack up in every one of those areas when compared with index funds and ETFs.

Your broker should be willing to openly discuss all those points and assess the risks of everything in which you invest. If you ask these questions and your broker starts talking about great managers beating the market, you will know that your broker has just changed the subject. This is not a sign that your needs and desires are being taken seriously.

_ This applies to me.
- [ ] Priority A
- [ ] Priority B
- [ ] Priority C

If you aren't entirely happy with your broker but you aren't ready to terminate the relationship, here's something you might try: Set up an account with a small part of your portfolio, perhaps 10 percent, at Vanguard and use it to invest according to my recommendations using either index funds or ETFs. Be sure to let the broker know this, as it will put him or her on notice that you mean business and you won't be a good future candidate for high-commission products.

If you do that, you might be amazed at how much more interested your broker has become about your beliefs and your desires.

77. Will you choose an advisor with a solo practice, doing everything, or one who has a support staff and works with other advisors?

I have a lot of admiration for advisors who do everything, because that encompasses a lot of territory: marketing and sales, trading, back-office administration, research, client service, collections, accounting, keeping abreast of changes in financial markets, and of course regulatory concerns.

A good advisor should have an overall grasp of all those areas, but the best advisor in my view is one who specializes in taking care of clients.

When the market is in turmoil and you are upset, you want an advisor who's available to you, not one who is too busy making trades and keeping on top of paperwork.

_ This applies to me.
- ☐ Priority A
- ☐ Priority B
- ☐ Priority C

And when you need to buy or sell, or you need help with paperwork, you want somebody who can help you now, not somebody who is busy advising other clients or who's out of the office for vacation or sick leave.

78. Will you instruct your advisor to put all your investments into index funds, or will you accept your advisor's choices for actively managed funds for some or all of your money?

The lure of beating the market is very powerful. Despite the overwhelming evidence that index funds are more efficient and productive, many advisors work exclusively with actively managed funds, believing they can identify the funds and managers who are most likely to outperform index funds. I have never seen any evidence that anybody can consistently do that.

Other advisors take what might be considered a hybrid approach. They prescribe index funds for what they consider the "core" asset classes, then choose active managers for a handful of funds that they believe will boost the portfolio's return.

I think the right answer is to stick with index funds. When you do that, you accept the returns of the market instead of trying to beat those returns. Once you have done that, your job as an investor is much easier and more likely to be successful.

_ This applies to me.
- ☐ Priority A
- ☐ Priority B
- ☐ Priority C

In spite of my arguments and the massive evidence of University Street, the siren song of active management is a hard lesson to learn. The majority of investors have to learn it through unfortunate – and expensive – experience.

79. Will you choose a local advisor or one who is far from your home?

I could make the case for either choice, and in the end it will depend on various factors. In general, your advisor's competence, beliefs and level of service will all be more important than the location of his or her office.

Technology has made long-distance communication feel as if it's local. The advisors at the company I started 30 years ago, take care of clients throughout the United States, and about half of them have never set foot in the firm's Seattle office. I believe this indicates that distance isn't a necessary barrier to getting good advice and service. Modern teleconferencing makes it possible to use personal computers to communicate over thousands of miles while preserving the feel of sitting across the desk.

It's quite easy to link distant computers so you can see what's on your advisor's screen, just as if he or she turned the screen your way in an office. This works so well that many people use teleconferencing even when they're in the same city.

On the other hand, your relationship with your financial advisor is quite personal, and there's no question that there's value in meeting face- to-face. This might be especially important for a couple in which one partner is much more involved than the other. If you are part of such a couple, and if you're reading this book, I'm pretty confident that you are the one who's more involved.

If you want your partner to continue the relationship with your advisor in case something should happen to you, then it's important to make sure your partner has at least some relationship with the advisor. In theory, that should work equally well over long distances as it does in local relationships. But in real life, a personal relationship that is based on at least some face-to-face contact is likely to be more enduring. So you may want to take this into consideration.

—This applies to me.
☐ Priority A
☐ Priority B
☐ Priority C

In the end, you'll have to weigh the various pros and cons. In order to qualify this as a $1,000 decision, I'll say this: Choose your advisor primarily on the basis of the knowledge, guidance, service and support you'll get.

If you find the right combination close to home, then so much the better. But if the choice is between competence and convenience, choose the former every time.

80. When you are evaluating the performance of an advisor, is one year a long enough period, or should you look farther back in time?

Over the almost 30 years of building our firm, I have talked to many new clients who planned to try our management services for a year, and see how they do in comparison with part of their portfolio they are managing on their own. On the surface, this seems like a sensible approach. If you can drive a new car for a year, or live in a new home for a year, you will have plenty of information to know if you want to make the arrangement permanent.

But investing isn't quite that easy. Anybody who has studied the markets knows that in the space of one year, anything can happen. If I'm your advisor and my investment choices happen to be spectacularly better performers than yours for a 12-month period, does that prove anything? Probably not. If yours are spectacularly better for 12 months, does that mean anything? Unfortunately, no.

During the roaring bull market of the late 1990s, the Standard & Poor's 500 Index was rolling along at more than 25 percent a year. Some people thought that "proved" that the index was better than the worldwide diversification we preached and practiced. Our worldwide portfolios performed well in that period, but their returns were less than half that of the S&P 500 Index.

—This applies to me.
☐   Priority A
☐   Priority B
☐   Priority C

One or two years of performance data doesn't tell you anything about the quality of a strategy or the quality of an advisor or fund manager. Millions of investors learned that the hard way in the decade starting in 2000, when our worldwide approach far outperformed the S&P 500 Index by over 7 percent a year.

81. Should you judge the quality of an advisor on your investment returns, or on something else?

Advisors are often judged by how much money their clients make, but that is a false grading system. Advisors do not make (or lose) money for their clients. Clients make money in the market and lose money to the market.

The quality of an advisor will show up in other ways. An advisor really earns his or her stripes by keeping you on course when you want to bail out in the bad times or load up on hot assets in the good times. An excellent advisor will be valuable by seeing that your accounts are rebalanced regularly so you keep your risk under control. He or she will do many other things that don't sound very glamorous, but will make a big long-term difference. A good advisor will apply smart tax- loss harvesting strategies and will encourage you to invest in dwindling markets when prices are declining, even though you won't feel like it. A good advisor will help you determine your need for return and the right amount of risk to take.

And an excellent advisor will teach you how to make the decisions and cultivate the attitudes and habits that will maximize your chances for success. You may have to wait five or 10 years, or even more, to realize the full payoff.

—This applies to me.
☐ Priority A
☐ Priority B
☐ Priority C

These things are much more important in the long run than short-term performance.

I have seen far too many investors spend most of their lives searching for a strategy that works all the time. That strategy doesn't exist. We all know what worked recently, but that readily available knowledge isn't worth much. There is no historical data that suggests investing in the latest "hot" idea is a productive guide to the future, even though it sure feels like it should be.

Part 7: **Insurance**

82. Should you buy long-term-care insurance, and if so, when?

This is a very complex topic. If you are seriously considering buying this insurance, I suggest you get professional help to make sure you look at all the relevant factors. Your best decision will depend in part on your present and anticipated financial resources. And it will depend on how strongly you want to avoid being a burden to your family or society.

I can't give you the full answer, but I can cover some points for you to think about. One scary fact is that the average cost of long-term care is about $80,000 a year, and it's expected to triple in the next 20 years.

One reason this insurance is so expensive is an arcane (but very real) concept known as adverse selection. This is the tendency of people who think they'll need the insurance to buy it while those who don't think they will need it opt out. An example that's easy to understand is health insurance. Group insurance, which requires everybody in the group to have coverage, is much less expensive because younger people and healthier people pay alongside those with higher risks.

If each person in a group, for instance every employee of a company, could decide whether or not to buy insurance, young people and healthy people would tend to opt out. But those with known health problems or risk factors would tend to opt in. In other words, the people who were most likely to collect would buy insurance while those least likely to collect would not buy it.

This is one reason that everybody in an employee pool must be covered by group policies.

Long-term-care coverage, since it is optional, is more likely to be purchased by people who believe they'll need it. From the insurance ₛ point of view, this makes these policies particularly risky. ₛ one reason the premiums can be very high.

As a start, the experts suggest you not pay any more than 7 percent or 8 percent of your income on LTC premiums. If you can't afford that, you may be better off taking the risk of running out of money, because you simply don't have enough to buy the protection you need.

One good online resource is the LTC Insurance Evaluator at ~~Smartmoney.com~~. It will help you go through all the choices involved in this coverage, including the option to insure yourself.

—This applies to me.
☐ Priority A
☐ Priority B
☐ Priority C

One of my favorite sources of insurance is USAA. You can visit them at USAA.com. Many of their products, including LTC coverage, are available even to non-members at discounted rates.

83. How much life insurance should you have?

One common rule of thumb is to have coverage equal to eight to 10 times your annual pay. Some people may need a lot more than that. Others may not need life insurance at all. If nothing else, this rule is a convenient way for insurance agents to convince prospective customers they need lots of life insurance.

The primary rationale for having life insurance is to protect whoever would suffer financial hardship if you were to die. If you don't have dependents, you might not need life insurance. If you have a disabled spouse or child, you might need lots of coverage.

To do a really good job of figuring this out, you need to think carefully about the people you are protecting and what needs you assume they would have upon your death. It's a good idea to plan as if you were going to die this week, instead of thinking about what they would need if you died after another 10 or 20 or 30 years.

To illustrate how a typical analysis might go, imagine you are a husband with a wife who stays at home to take care of the kids. What would happen if you suddenly died? Normally there are several phases of your family's life that would need to be funded. For some number of years, the kids would remain home and your wife might or might not return to work. When the kids were of college age, would you want enough life insurance to pay their tuition? (Remember that if your answer is yes, you're talking about very large sums of money.)

When the kids were gone, there would be a period of some years before your wife was eligible for Social Security retirement benefits. Could she support herself in these years, or do you want enough insurance that she won't have to work more than part-time, or not at all? After she's retired, do you want enough insurance money left to supplement her pension and Social Security?

Do you want the mortgage paid off right away? Other debts too? Should your wife have an emergency fund, and if so, how big should it be? Would your parents and/or your wife's parents be able and willing to help with their grandchildren's education?

There are so many factors at work in this decision that you may find it worthwhile to consult an advisor or financial planner. My preference would be somebody who doesn't sell insurance, for obvious reasons.

It's easy to get carried away, thinking that life insurance can cover a myriad of potential future needs. All that insurance is expensive, and the premiums you pay takes money that instead could be going into savings or making your family's life better right now. If you buy too little insurance, you could wind up leaving your family with a big problem. But if you buy too much, you'll be misusing your financial resources.

—This applies to me.
☐ Priority A
☐ Priority B
☐ Priority C

Short of engaging the services of a professional, you can go online to smartmoney.com and use their life insurance calculator.

84. Should you buy whole life insurance or term insurance?

Most financial experts who don't sell insurance are in favor of buying term instead of whole life. They believe that whole life insurance is an awful investment. I agree. If you need insurance, get pure insurance. If you need an investment or savings, get that somewhere besides an insurance company.

Term insurance is a simple contract between you and the insurance company. You pay a premium for a given number of years, which can be one to 30, and the company will pay the face amount of the policy if you die during the life or "term" of the contract. If you live until the end of the term, the insurance company pays nothing.

From the company's point of view, the real cost of this insurance naturally goes up as you get older and your chances of dying increase. In order to reflect this reality, the premium typically goes up with every renewal. A one-year renewable term policy can start out with a relatively low premium, which increases a little bit every year.

Now consider a 10-year term life insurance policy with a fixed premium for that whole period. The real cost to the insurance company will go up every year as you get older, but the company can't raise the price. Therefore, the premium must be set high enough at the outset that it will cover all the years in the policy. In effect this means you'll overpay for the "real" cost of the coverage in the early years and eventually you'll underpay in the last years.

Now think about a "whole life" policy in which the insurance company agrees to cover your death no matter how long you live, and you agree to pay a fixed premium from the start. If you buy such a policy in your 20s, the premium may seem very low. But that premium is carefully calculated, knowing that your chances of dying in the early years of the policy are very low.

In reality, you will be overpaying for life insurance for most of the life of the contract. Your overpayments do two things. First, they help subsidize the insurance company's cost when older policyholders pass away. Second, they let the company refund part of those overpayments to you in the form of "dividends" that can reduce your future premiums or be kept for you in what amounts to a savings account.

The existence of this savings account, which you can tap only in very limited circumstances unless you drop the policy, allows insurance companies to sell whole life policies as investments. However, the return on these "investments" is far too low to be worthwhile, in my opinion.

If you're 30 years old and in good health, you may be able to buy a $100,000 whole-life policy for $100 a month. The premium will never rise, and when you're in your 70s, that will be a very attractive price. But in the meantime, you'll be paying way too much. How do you know this? Because for less than $20 a month you may be able to buy the same amount of coverage in a 30-year term policy.

If you buy the term policy and put the $80 a month you save into buying a boat, it's hard to see how you have improved your financial situation. (In fact, doing that might actually hurt your situation, because boats have a way of demanding more money over the years than most new boat owners ever count on.) But if you use the $80 monthly savings to add to your retirement savings, you have enhanced your future financial fitness.

—This applies to me.
☐ Priority A
☐ Priority B
☐ Priority C

Insurance salespeople understand all this very well, yet they work tirelessly to sell whole life insurance. If you wonder why, consider the motivation of receiving a commission of as much as 100 percent of the first year's premium on a whole-life policy, vs. perhaps 20 percent of the (much lower) first-year premium on a term policy.

If you were selling insurance, would you work harder to earn 100 percent of $1,200 than you would to earn only 20 percent of $240? I thought so!

Part 8: Retirement accounts and planning for retirement

85. Should you annuitize your pension, or take a lump sum and roll it over into an IRA?

For many people this is one of the biggest financial decisions they will ever make. If you annuitize your pension, you agree to accept a contract from an insurance company, which will pay you monthly income for the rest of your life no matter how long you live. You may have the option to choose a reduced monthly amount and have it continue until both you and your spouse have passed away. The payments may be fixed in their dollar amounts, or they may start at a lower amount that will rise annually to account for future inflation. The biggest attraction of choosing an annuity is that you know that you won't run out of income, and you can let the insurance company worry about how to invest the money.

If you choose to take a lump sum, you assume the responsibility for investing the money and for your choice of how much to withdraw for your living expenses. If you do either one of these things poorly, you could potentially run out of money.

One big factor in the decision is your life expectancy. If you expect to live into your 90s or beyond, the annuity becomes very attractive. If your health is poor, on the other hand, you may want to take the lump sum.

Another important factor is your need for income. An annuity is likely to pay considerably more than you could get by investing the same number of dollars in a bond fund. This makes the annuity an attractive choice for cautious investors with a high need for income. On the other hand, if you're able to get along on an uncertain or variable income, taking a lump sum and investing it well has the potential for higher returns through a combination of stock funds and bond funds.

In addition to that, if you take the lump sum, whatever principal is left at the end of your life is yours to leave in your will. If you annuitize, the principal immediately becomes the property of the insurance company.

You can see that this decision has a number of important aspects. One factor to consider is the financial health of your employer. If you annuitize your pension and your company goes bankrupt, your pension is likely insured by the federal Pension Benefit Guaranty Corporation, up to $4,500 per month.

Because the ramifications of this decision can be complex, and because a decision to take an annuity is permanent and irrevocable, if you aren't sure what to do, I suggest you consult a financial advisor who can help you make sure you are aware of all the potential consequences in your choice.

The potential disaster that I worry about is people who are overconfident that they can invest to beat the market. In the great bull market of the late 1990s, many people believed that investing was pretty easy and that they could rely on getting long-term returns of 20 to 30 percent. A lot of those people took more risk than they realized they were taking, lost half or more of their money, and then became extremely conservative. I hope you will spare yourself such unnecessary financial drama.

You may want to take your pension in cash and use some of it to buy your own annuity. If you do that, an advisor can help you find one with low costs. Both Vanguard and USAA have very fine products that are commission-free. (Many USAA products are restricted to people who have served in the armed forces, but, contrary to what many people believe, USAA annuities are available to any investor.)

—This applies to me.
☐   Priority A
☐   Priority B
☐   Priority C

86.   Should you retire when you have enough in savings that you can meet your needs with distributions of 4 percent a year, or should you keep working to build up your savings even more?

This is a big decision, and the answer depends partly on the state of your health and your life expectancy – and partly on the relative strengths of your desires to keep working vs. to retire. I assume from your question that you have a choice about it, and that is a very good position for you to be in.

The financial component involves a tradeoff between money now and money later. If you save more now, you'll have more to spend later. I'm always in favor of over-saving, because I have seen the additional freedom that gives people to live their lives the way they want to. (Obviously if that extra saving requires you to continue working in a job you dislike, this detracts from your quality of life.)

When you retire with more, you not only have higher balances but you have fewer years in which your savings will need to support you. That gives you the option of withdrawing a higher percentage of your assets. Here are two simple examples. Scenario 1: Assume that you need $20,000 a year from your portfolio. If you have saved $500,000, you can take out 4 percent per year and, at relatively little risk of ever running out of money, adjust that amount upward every year to cover inflation. Scenario 2: With the same need for $20,000, assume you have saved $1 million. With this much cushion, you can increase your withdrawal rate to 5 percent and take out $50,000 a year, knowing that if your investments fall on tough times you could cut back to the $20,000. This second scenario, the result of saving more than is necessary, puts you in great shape.

The bottom line for me is that over-saving usually adds to peace of mind in retirement. Just make sure that you use some of your savings to enjoy your life while you can, because the future for each of us is uncertain. Even if you have 10 times as much money as you need, if you don't let yourself enjoy it until your health deteriorates, your extra savings may not give you the rewards that you deserve.

—This applies to me.
☐   Priority A
☐   Priority B
☐   Priority C

87. What percentage of your income should you expect to need in planning for retirement?

I believe it's prudent to assume you'll need as much income after you retire as you had before you retired. Many experts suggest you plan for only 80 percent, since you won't have to pay commuting and other work-related costs and you'll no longer need to be saving for retirement.

All that's true, but after you retire you are likely to have more time available for hobbies, travel and other pursuits, all of which may cost money you weren't spending while you were working. In addition, your health-care costs are likely to go up as you get older.

—This applies to me.
☐   Priority A
☐   Priority B
☐   Priority C

88.   If you're over 70 and must take required minimum distributions from your 401(k) account even though you don't need this money to live on, where should you invest what's left over after paying taxes?

Here's a case in which you can adopt any answer that suits you, except that you won't be able to put it back into the 401(k) account.

If it's money you don't think you'll need to live on, and if you already have adequate cash reserves for emergencies and opportunities, then I suggest you think about what you intend for that money eventually.

If the money will someday go to your children or grandchildren, consider investing it with their needs and their risk tolerance in mind. (Their risk tolerance is probably greater than yours, by the way.) You could also think about giving them some of the money now, while you are alive to witness their enjoyment of it and to help them learn from whatever they do with the money.

If the money will someday go to charity, consider giving some of it now for a tax deduction that you can enjoy. You'll presumably get the satisfaction of seeing your money put to good use. And if the numbers are big enough, maybe you can get a new building or a scholarship named after yourself or somebody important to you.

—This applies to me.
☐ Priority A
☐ Priority B
☐ Priority C

If you don't have a particular use in mind for this money, then I suggest you invest it similarly to the rest of your portfolio, at moderate risk levels. That should keep all your options open.

89.   When you evaluate past rates of inflation, should you look at actual inflation year by year, or accept the average rates over long periods of time?

I think accepting average rates is a trap. Inflation has not gone up and down nearly as dramatically as investment returns, but inflation doesn't occur at a fixed rate, either. In broad terms, interest rates and rates of inflation often seem to go up and down together, though they are rarely in lock-step.

If you looked at stock and bond returns for the 42 years 1970 through 2011 and used an assumed inflation rate of 3 or 3.5 percent, you might come to the conclusion that you would have been in great shape. But if you applied the real rates of inflation in the sequence in which they really happened, you would see that investors who relied heavily on fixed-income funds sometimes had a very tough time keeping up with inflation.

—This applies to me.
☐ Priority A
☐ Priority B
☐ Priority C

Though we know the history of inflation, we don't know it's future. Inflation could be very benign, or it could rage seemingly out of control, robbing savers of their purchasing power. Use actual past rates, not long-term averages.

90.   What rate of inflation should you assume for the future?

Although in the short term inflation can seem like a non-issue, it can bite investors and retirees pretty severely, sometimes with little or no advance notice. The conservative approach, of course, is to estimate high.

In the 80 years ending December 2011, the actual inflation rate was 3.5 percent. For the trailing 25-year and 50-year periods, inflation was 2.9% and 4.1% respectively. That gives you a range of what might be reasonable to expect.

Future inflation will either be higher, the same, or lower than it has been. If I had to predict, I would predict that inflation will be a bit higher than it has been in recent years. I recommend that you plan for retirement based on the assumption that inflation will be at least 3.5 percent. If you can manage to save enough to keep up with 4 percent future inflation, that's even better. That rate is only possible as that was the rate from 1941-2011

Many people who have studied this topic believe the real inflation that most of us experience is far higher than the rates that are widely reported. From 1955 through 1969, inflation was 2.3 percent, a figure that seems quite mild. At the end of that period, you needed $35,162 to purchase what $25,000 would have bought 15 years earlier. If all you had was a fixed annuity, you were in trouble.

—This applies to me.
☐ Priority A
☐ Priority B
☐ Priority C

And things got worse. In the following 15 years, inflation heated up considerably. In 1984, you needed $69,949 to purchase what $25,000 would have bought 15 years earlier, in 1969.

91. Should you save for retirement in an IRA, or use a 401(k)?

Ideally, you will do both. If you have a 401(k) or similar plan available where you work, I think it should get first claim on your retirement dollars, at least until you have contributed enough to qualify for anything your company will match. Even if there's no match, an employer-sponsored retirement plan gives you automatic savings and the long-term benefits of dollar-cost averaging.

On the other hand, most 401(k) plans fall short of giving employees access to all the asset classes I think they should have. Therefore, after you have qualified for the maximum matching funds from your employer, I suggest you use an IRA to invest in the asset classes that may be missing from your 401(k) or similar plan.

So, to summarize, the first priority is the 401(k) to obtain matching funds. If you can save more, the second priority is an IRA to pick up missing asset classes. After you have maximized your ability to contribute to an IRA, if you have still more that you can invest, either put it into your 401(k) for its tax deferral or put it into a taxable account for the superior investment choices that will open up for you.

—This applies to me.
☐ Priority A
☐ Priority B
☐ Priority C

92. Should your 401(k) or IRA be invested in a target-date retirement fund, or should you build your own customized portfolio?

Target-date funds provide an easy solution to a tough problem. Notice I chose the word "easy" and not the word "good." The problem is the need to change your asset mix as you get closer to retirement. The target-date- fund's solution is to automatically move assets from stocks to bonds as the fund gets closer to its specified target date.

This solution is better than investing in stock funds when you're young and never moving to bond funds. And because most target-date funds have a lot of diversification, it's better than investing in only a few asset classes or (even worse) only a few individual stocks.

Most people have little knowledge of how to be successful long-term investors, and target-date funds can combine professional stock picking, asset allocation and automatic rebalancing, all things that are beneficial to investors. What's not to like about that?

As it turns out, these funds have several drawbacks. In your retirement savings, your objective should be to squeeze out every bit of return you can get without taking undue risk. Target funds don't do that. Instead, they leave too much additional return on the table.
They tend to own too much in fixed-income for young investors, and on the equity side they have too little in international, small cap, value, emerging markets, and real estate. To top it off, some target-date funds have outrageously high expenses.
My recommendation is that you skip these funds in favor of a customized portfolio, which I believe can add one to two percentage points to your annual return without adding risk. That is potentially a life-changing difference.

—This applies to me.
☐ Priority A
☐ Priority B
☐ Priority C

93. Should you invest 10 percent or more of your 401(k) in the stock of your company, or not?

"Not" is the right answer here.

Investing heavily in company stock is a common way that investors take too much risk without getting paid any premium return for doing so. When you're already relying on one company for your income and your health insurance (and if you're lucky, a pension too), loading up your portfolio with that company's stock is increasing your risk exponentially.

Academics who have studied this have come to the conclusion that you would need to get four to five times the return of the Standard & Poor's 500 Index in order to justify the higher risk of betting your portfolio on just a single company.

—This applies to me.
☐   Priority A
☐   Priority B
☐   Priority C

I've known many people who were sure their own company was the exception to this rule, and I've heard too many tales of shocked disappointment. I don't want to hear yours added to the list.

94. Is there a sensible way that you can increase the risk you're taking in your 401(k) in the hopes of gaining a higher return?

In general, I am reluctant to recommend ramping up your risk in order to boost your return. My objection isn't to the idea, which can make sense. My problem is the many foolish things people do when they are hoping to hit a home run.

If you can avoid that dangerous temptation, there is a sensible approach that's worth considering. Start by properly diversifying the great majority of your portfolio, say 90 percent, and then concentrate the final 10 percent in an asset class with a long history of excess returns – or maybe do this with two such asset classes.

—This applies to me.
☐   Priority A
☐   Priority B
☐   Priority C

Two asset classes that come to mind immediately are small-cap value stocks and emerging market stocks. As a group, small-cap value stocks have earned three or four extra percentage points of long-term return, compared with the S&P 500 Index. That's enough to make an enormous difference. Emerging markets, while their returns are very volatile, have had a high long-term return.

To implement this approach, include these two asset classes at their normal percentage weightings in the 90 percent of your portfolio that is fully diversified. Then concentrate the final 10 percent in U.S. and international small-cap value stocks and emerging markets stocks. If you do that, I think you'll have a good shot at adding some extra return over the years.

This is vastly more sensible than loading up on one or two stocks, which so many people do. There are many examples of individual companies failing unexpectedly (remember Enron and Washington Mutual). But there's never been an entire asset class that went broke.

95. Should you start taking Social Security as soon as possible, or wait until you have used up your other resources?

This is one of those decisions that in my opinion should be made with the help of a good advisor, because everybody's situation is different and there can be a lot of "moving parts" that should be considered. The basic decision is fairly simple. If you need the money to live on and you don't have a good alternative, then start collecting. If you are eligible for Social Security and your health isn't good (so you don't expect to live a long life), then start collecting.
If you don't need the money right away and your health is good, you'll get higher monthly benefits if you wait until you're 70. This might be particularly beneficial if you have a younger spouse who is likely to outlive you and who would benefit from receiving your benefit after you are gone.

Some people start collecting benefits as soon as they are eligible because they're worried that Social Security will run out of money. I don't know any more than anybody else about the future of Social Security. The experts say that if no changes are made to the system, current tax revenues suggest that the Social Security trust fund will be in serious trouble by the year 2037. The future of this system cannot be known, and I certainly don't blame investors for being concerned.

If you can adequately cover your cost of living in the years from 62 to 70 without taking Social Security, your benefits will go up about 8 percent for every year you wait. To my mind that seems like an 8 percent pay raise. How long has it been since you got a raise like that?

—This applies to me.
☐ Priority A
☐ Priority B
☐ Priority C

The decision becomes more complex when a spouse is added to the mix. Sometimes it makes sense for the spouse with a lower earnings history to start taking benefits at age 62. Sometimes it makes sense for the spouse with a higher earnings history to choose a "file-and-suspend" option that lets the lower-paid spouse collect partial benefits.

96. Where should you go for more information on Social Security benefits?

Most of what you need to know about Social Security can be found online at ssa.gov.org. You can log on to get access to your own records and quickly determine the benefits that you would get at various ages. In my own case, at 68, I could start collecting benefits of $2,569 a month. But if I wait until I'm 70, my payment would go up to $3,138, an increase of 22 percent. That seems like a good deal to me, but of course it will only be a good deal if I live long enough to make up for the months that I didn't take $2,569.

Here's one other thing you should know about Social Security: If you were previously married, you may be eligible to receive benefits based on your former spouse's benefits. The government won't contact you to tell you about this, so you may want to inquire at a local Social Security office.

—This applies to me.
☐ Priority A
☐ Priority B
☐ Priority C

97. When you're planning your retirement savings, what rate should you assume that your investments will earn?

This seems like a very simple question, a small item. But it matters a great deal. If you assume a high rate of return, you could save too little money and eventually wind up with too few resources to take care of yourself and your family. If on the other hand you assume a very low rate of return, you might become discouraged and not save at all, or you might try to save so much that you deprive your family of resources they need for other things. So it's worthwhile to try to get this right.

Most advisors use historical returns of various asset allocations to evaluate the returns that are likely at different levels of investment risk. I suggest you assume future returns would be 1 to 2 percent less than those shown in the following table. So, if a 50/50 combination of stock funds and bond funds produced 9 percent in the past, you should base your planning on 7 to 8 percent in the future.

—This applies to me.
☐ Priority A
☐ Priority B
☐ Priority C

Hypothetical returns of balanced asset class portfolios (1970-2011)

Equity portion is 50% US/ 50% International.

This isn't based on any knowledge of the future. Instead it's based on a healthy conservative point of view that I believe is wise. If returns are higher, you'll be able to deal with that "problem."

	Fixed Income	10% Equity	20% Equity	30% Equity	40% Equity	50% Equity	60% Equity	70% Equity	80% Equity	90% Equity	100% Equity	S&P Index w/divs
Annualized Return	6.5	7.0	7.5	8.0	8.5	9.0	9.5	10.0	10.5	11.0	11.5	12.0
Worst Year	(4.8)	(4.5)	(6.5)	(8.6)	(10.7)	(12.8)	(14.9)	(17.1)	(19.2)	(21.3)	(23.4)	(21.5)

98. If you are a teacher, should you use a variable annuity inside of your 403(b) retirement plan so you are guaranteed not to lose money?

The short answer is no, you shouldn't.

Now I will give you the longer answer. A variable annuity is a contract with an insurance company in which you make periodic payments or a lump-sum payment into a tax-deferred account. Under the umbrella of the variable annuity you are offered a variety of fixed-income, equity, and balanced portfolios that are similar to mutual funds.

The fees within a variable annuity can range from 2% to 3% a year, which is very high for investing in funds. The fees are sometimes rationalized as the cost of deferring taxes. But this is a phony argument when a salesperson is advocating an annuity inside a retirement plan that is already tax-deferred or tax-free. The high fees hurt you while they help the salesperson and the insurance company, and you get little in return.

—This applies to me.
☐   Priority A
☐   Priority B
☐   Priority C

Vanguard sells variable annuities but specifically advises against putting them in qualified tax-deferred accounts.

99. When the insurance company guarantees that you can't lose money in an annuity, isn't that a great safety factor to have in your retirement plan?

It's true that a variable annuity comes with a guarantee that if you die while you still hold the account, your estate will get at least as much as you invested. So technically you cannot lose money. But how much is that guarantee worth?

History indicates the insurance company takes almost no risk by making this guarantee. The company isn't betting on the future of just one stock but on a diversified portfolio that has never in history suffered a permanent bear market. When we study balanced portfolios with 60 percent in equities and 40 percent in bonds from 1927 through 2011, we can't find a single 10-year period in which such a portfolio lost money.

It's almost certain the insurance company won't pay anything for making this guarantee. But it is guaranteed that the customer will pay more, and thus get a lower return, because of this provision.

I have always been amazed at how the insurance industry can fool so many smart teachers into thinking that an overpriced product like a variable annuity is a good deal. And I'm amazed at how school districts, colleges and universities accept the insurance industry's retirement choices.

Instead of investing in a variable annuity, I hope you will consider using one of the Vanguard portfolios I recommend. That should give you a huge advantage over variable annuities. I also recommend that you read the U.S. Securities and Exchange Commission report "Variable Annuities: What You Should Know." It includes five warnings that should steer you in a different direction.

—This applies to me.
☐ Priority A
☐ Priority B
☐ Priority C

100. If your employer allows it, should you borrow money from your 401(k) plan, knowing that you'll be able to pay it back and knowing that even though you will pay interest on the loan, that interest will go to you?

Unless you are facing a true emergency and there are no alternatives open to you (this would be very rare), borrowing from your 401(k) is a bad idea. That's spelled b-a-d, as in bad. Don't do it!

This idea is bad primarily for two reasons: practicality and taxes. On the practical side, you will probably find it onerous to pay back the money you borrowed, as the payments will be deducted from your paychecks. In addition, until the loan is paid back you can't contribute more money to your retirement account. That costs you a tax deduction and possibly a match from your employer.

If you took the maximum five-year period to repay the loan, you would permanently lose the opportunity to set aside more than $82,000 in a tax-deferred account.

The bigger dangers in taking out a 401(k) loan involve taxes.

In a best-case scenario, you will successfully repay the money to your retirement plan, along with the interest that you owe to yourself. There is no tax deduction for these repayments, including the interest. You will pay that interest with dollars that have already been taxed. That may seem fair, but there's a catch: After you retire, every dollar you take out of the account will be taxed at your highest marginal tax rate, including the interest you previously paid.

That means that the money you paid in interest will be taxed twice: once when you earned it from your employer (it's coming out of your salary) and again when you take it out. If you are in the 25 percent marginal tax bracket, your tax burden on that money could become 50 percent.

It's true the interest you pay will be at a low rate, and the number of dollars won't be high. But paying taxes twice on the same dollars is contrary to everything I try to teach people about using their money efficiently and making it work for them, not somebody else.

That's the best-case scenario.

But think for a moment about what happens if for any reason you were to lose your job before the loan was repaid. Although the details can vary depending on your employer's specific plan, it's very likely that as soon as you are no longer employed, the balance of the loan plus accrued interest will be due and payable within 60 days.

When you are suddenly out of a job, do you think you will have enough extra cash readily available to write a check to the 401(k) plan and pay off the loan?

If you don't repay the loan, the outstanding balance, including interest, will be treated as a distribution from the account. As such, it will be added to your taxable income. If you are not yet 59½ years old, you may be slapped with a 10 percent early withdrawal penalty in addition to taxes.

—This applies to me.
☐ Priority A
☐ Priority B
☐ Priority C

A 401(k) loan can become an extremely expensive way to borrow money, and except in very unusual circumstances, it's a bad idea. Therefore the right answer to this question is No!

Part 9: Forward into the Future

101. Is simply reading this workbook enough to improve your financial fitness, or should you do something?

WHAT A QUESTION! Reading this guide is a good step, but all the knowledge and understanding in the world won't do you any good unless you put it to work.

This is a workbook, and I hope you have used it by marking topics that warrant your attention. Now you have come to the part where the rubber meets the road. Will you move to action? I certainly hope so.

Use the following page to note the items you flagged earlier, and then write a simple action step or two for each of your top priorities. After you have done that, I hope you'll set aside at least one hour a week to tackle the topics that are most likely to boost your financial fitness.

—This applies to me.
☐ Priority A
☐ Priority B
☐ Priority C

If you do this diligently every week, I'm comfortable in predicting that sometime in the future you will regard that one-hour-a-week as time that was very well spent.

A Note from Paul

I've done my best to address the important topics and give you enough information to move ahead. I invite you to join me at my website and social media to keep apprised of current recommendations, podcasts, articles, and other news.

I am always open to questions, and you are welcome to contact me at PM@paulmerriman.com. Please include your phone number so I can contact you to clarify your situation and questions. Sometimes, the best way to arrive at the right answer is by having a discussion.

Paul A. Merriman

Appendix A: **Asset Allocation**

In this appendix I introduce you to some of the many asset allocation approaches you can use to determine the best balance of fixed income and equity investments to meet your needs. This discussion is aimed at arriving at only two numbers: the percentage you'll hold in stock funds and the percentage in fixed-income funds. (They should add up to 100, so in fact we might be looking for only one number.) If those numbers are 60 and 40, respectively, then 60 percent of your portfolio is allocated to various stock funds and the other 40 percent to fixed-income. I recommend, and for this discussion I assume, that you will diversify your assets properly within each of these two parts of your portfolio.

Here are 10 approaches to finding the right balance.

1. I always like investment decisions that can be made automatically, without letting our emotions take over. An often-cited asset allocation formula asks you to subtract your age from 100 and then put that percentage into stock funds, with the rest going to bonds. Stated another way, your current age tells you the percentage you should hold in bonds. This is easy to calculate and very conservative because it uses a hefty dosage of bonds even for young investors. I think it's too conservative. It seeks to protect young investors from falling stock prices (30 percent in bonds for a 30-year-old) even though falling stock prices can be beneficial to people who are putting money aside. And this formula deprives older retirees of some of the equities I think they need in order to keep up with inflation.

2. The previous formula can be improved by subtracting your age from 110 or 120 instead of 100. This will give you an additional 10 to 20 percentage points in equities, and over time I believe that is likely to add 0.5 to 1 percentage points to your return. That may seem insignificant, but over a lifetime it can easily add $500,000 to $1 million to your retirement savings.

3. I believe in defensive investment strategies, but defense is not necessarily the best approach when you are young. Young investors

who understand the benefits of bear markets for accumulators should have 100 percent of their retirement investments in a diversified portfolio of equities. However, their portfolios should become less aggressive as they get older.

Here's a simple formula for doing that, one I think can work well for many people: When you reach age 35, move 10 percent (if you consider yourself aggressive) or 20 percent (if you feel conservative) of your portfolio into bond funds. Every five years after that, move another 5 percent of your portfolio into bond funds. At age 65, this leaves an aggressive investor with 40 percent in bonds and a conservative investor with 50 percent in bonds. Those are good allocations that many retirees can live with the rest of their lives.

4. Another legitimate asset allocation approach for the rest of your life is to invest in a target-date retirement fund. Vanguard has low-cost entries in this category. This approach is as simple and automatic as it gets. One decision lasts for life. But there's a cost for this simplicity. I believe investors in these funds will give up 1 percent to 2 percent in returns every year. Target-date funds tend to be over-weighted in fixed-income, and their equity holdings have too little exposure to international stocks, small-company stocks and value stocks.

If you're going to take this route, I strongly advise you to consult with a professional to make sure you get what's right for you. Target-date retirement funds assume that the only thing that determines your risk tolerance is the year you plan to retire. If only investing were that simple! When you buy a target-date fund, you are making one decision for life. Before you do that, I hope you will go to whatever trouble and expense is necessary to make sure it's a decision you can live with.

5. You might start by determining how much of your portfolio, in percentage terms, you believe you will be willing to lose without abandoning your long-term strategy, and then find the asset allocation "sweet spot" that would give you the highest return while keeping you within your range of risk tolerance. If you take this approach, I recommend you work with a professional investment advisor to periodically review your portfolio and talk about whether this is till the right long-term strategy for you.

6. Consider the inverse of what I just described. Start by figuring out how much long-term return you need in order to reach your goals, then use the Fine-Tuning Your Asset Allocation table to find the lowest-risk way to seek that return. One danger with this approach is that your desired or needed return may require too much risk for your comfort. This of course is where the rubber meets the road in asset allocation, and you may have to do some soul-searching to navigate through this territory.

I have talked to a lot of people who grappled with this situation, and my advice is unequivocal: Don't push yourself beyond your comfort zone in order to try to earn a high return. This will almost certainly lead you to abandon your strategy and wind up with less than if you had pursued a more moderate course. Instead, stay within your comfort zone and reduce your need for return by saving more, working longer, planning to live on less in retirement, or working part-time after you retire or quite likely some combination of those.

7. Some retired investors who are living off their income are spooked at the thought of having any of their money at all exposed to the risk of the stock market. Yet often they realize they need more inflation protection than they can get from fixed-income funds. If that describes you, consider the following approach, which has worked for many investors I know. Put enough of your portfolio into the bond funds that I recommend so that the interest meets your cash flow needs. The rest of your portfolio goes into stock funds. When inflation pushes your needs above the interest you get from the bond funds, supplement that income by withdrawing money from the stock funds.

Here's an example: The monthly-income portfolio I recommend, as I write this, has a current yield of 4.4 percent. Suppose you have a $1 million portfolio from which you need $35,000 a year. You can obtain that income by putting $800,000 into the four fixed-income funds, leaving $200,000 for stock funds.

8. If you have accumulated enough assets to meet your needs, for heaven's sake scale back your level of risk to become more defensive. You should do this even if you continue to work and add money to your portfolio. I think you should aspire to reach the ultimate in financial luxury, when you can take less risk and sleep soundly.

Unfortunately, many people have trouble knowing when enough is truly enough. By 1999, the technology bubble had produced sufficient wealth for many investors to retire without worry, even though they planned to keep on working. Many of them made the mistake of continuing to take unnecessary risks, which led to big (and unnecessary) losses in the bear market of 2000 through 2002. You may never reach the point where you're sure you have it made. But if you do, I hope you will scale back your risks so you don't have to start over building your wealth.

9. One of the most amazing things I have learned over the years is how readily an investor can turn a relatively conservative portfolio into a bonanza. Some years ago we wrote an article entitled "One Portfolio for Life" that advocated a lifetime allocation of 60 percent equity and 40 percent fixed income. Granted, this is probably too conservative for many investors in their 20s and 30s, and it may be too aggressive for many retirees. But I continue to think that this allocation, while not perfect, will protect investors from the worst ravages of bear markets and will give them the growth they need as they accumulate assets and the inflation protection they need when they are retired.

I studied this allocation back to 1927, and here's what I found: If you owned a portfolio that was 60% in diversified equities and 40 percent in five-year government bonds, your return was almost exactly the same as if you had owned only the S&P 500 Index -- with only about 40 percent of the risk. To measure this, we studied periods that lasted 120 months, or 10 years, and we used monthly returns. From 1927 through 2010, there were 877 10-year periods. We found that the S&P lost money in 53 of those periods. Let me say it again: There were 53 times when an investor in the U.S. stock market's premier index could look back over 10 years and find a loss. The 60/40 portfolio I just described never had one -- not even one -- losing 10-year period.

Actually, the story is even better for today's investors, who have easy access to more asset classes that have outperformed the S&P 500 while still reducing risk. For example, the 60 percent equity portfolio I just described returned 7.5% a year for the 10 years ending December 31, 2010; with the added asset classes I recommend, that portfolio returned 8.9% a year. Remember, those numbers cover a period that many people have called "the lost decade." Yes, this decade was lost for many investors. But those who diversified well, did well.

10.   Finally, I want to share something a bright young investor told me that kept him from throwing in the towel during the nasty 2007-2009 bear market. This man was 34, had a good job at a big technology company in California and had very good savings habits. I was startled to learn that he had been keeping 20 percent of his portfolio in the bond funds I had recommended over the years. I told him I couldn't believe that 20 percent in bonds was enough to keep him from losing a lot of money in the bear market. He agreed that it wasn't. But he told me that those bond funds kept him in the game because he knew he couldn't lose everything he had set aside for his future. If you think a similar approach will work for you, I encourage you to give it serious consideration.

I hope that somewhere in this list you will find an asset allocation strategy that will fit your own needs. No matter how much or how little you have invested, it's worth your while to find the right allocation formula to give you both peace of mind and a piece of the action. If you have that, then, in my book, you have it made.

Appendix A reprinted from "Financial Fitness Forever", courtesy of McGraw-Hill, publisher, copyright © 2012 by Paul Merriman and Richard Buck.

About the Authors:

Paul Merriman

Paul Merriman is nationally recognized as an authority on mutual funds, index investing, asset allocation and both buy-and-hold and active management strategies.

He is the founder of Paul A. Merriman & Associates, an investment advisory firm that is now Merriman LLC. The Seattle-based firm manages more than $1.5 billion for more than 2,000 households throughout the United States.

In his retirement, Paul remains passionately committed to educating and empowering investors. In 2012, he is working on the "How To Invest" series which distills his decades of expertise into concise investment books targeted to specific audiences.

Paul is also the author of four previous books on personal investing, including **Financial Fitness Forever: 5 Steps To More Money, Less Risk and More Peace of Mind** (McGraw Hill, Oct. 2011). The book was part of the "Financial Fitness Kit" offered on the TV show, "Financial Fitness After 50" that Paul created exclusively to raise funds for local Public Broadcasting Service (PBS) stations. The kit also included a workbook, six CDs and five DVDs.

Paul's book, **Live It Up Without Outliving Your Money! Creating The Perfect Retirement,** published by John Wiley & Sons, was released in an updated edition June 2008.

Over the years Paul has led more than 1,000 investor workshops, hosted a weekly radio program and has been a featured guest on local, regional and national television shows. Paul has written many articles for FundAdvice..com, a service of Merriman LLC. This Web site was identified by Forbes as one of the best online resources for investors.

Paul's weekly podcast, "Sound Investing," was named by *Money* magazine as the best money podcast. Paul has been widely quoted in national publications and has spoken to many local chapters of the American Association of Individual Investors (AAII). Twice he has been a featured guest speaker at Harvard University's investor psychology conference.

Paul began his career in the 1960s, working briefly as a broker for a major Wall Street firm. He concluded that Wall Street was burdened with too many conflicts of interest and decided to help small companies raise venture capital. In 1979, he became president and chairman of a public manufacturing company in the Pacific Northwest. He retired in 1982 to create his independent investment management firm.

Paul is the recipient of a distinguished alumni award from Western Washington University's School of Economics and is a founding member of the board of directors of Global HELP, a Seattle-based non-profit organization that produces medical publications and distributes them free to doctors and other health care workers in developing nations.

Paul donates all profits from the sales of his books to The Merriman Financial Educational Foundation, which is dedicated to providing comprehensive financial education to investors, with information and tools to make informed decisions in their own best interest and successfully implement their retirement savings program.

For questions and comments, Email: pm@paulmerriman.com

Richard Buck

Richard Buck was a Seattle Times business reporter for 20 years, capping a 30-year journalism career that included eight years as a writer and editor for The Associated Press. He began working with Paul in 1993 and retired in the fall of 2011 as senior editor of Merriman Inc. In that position he helped Paul and other Merriman staff members write many articles and was the ghostwriter for Paul's previous books, **Financial Fitness Forever** and **Live It Up Without Outliving Your Money!** in addition to the "How To Invest" Series.

Richard has also chosen to receive no compensation and to donate all profits from the sale of this series to a scholarship fund at his alma mater, Willamette University.

About the *How to Invest series*

Paul A. Merriman's **"How To Invest"** series provides concise and timeless information for creating a secure financial future and stress-free retirement. Each book addresses a specific audience or investor topic.

With almost 50 years of experience as a nationally recognized authority on mutual funds, asset allocation and retirement planning, Paul is an educator, committed to helping people of all ages and incomes make the most of their investments, with less risk and more peace of mind.

All profits from the sale of this series are donated to educational non-profit organizations.

The first book in the series, **First-Time Investor: Grow and Protect Your Money**, gives you easy-to-understand and follow steps necessary to start, build and maintain a successful investment portfolio for life that will lead to a secure retirement. If you have ever struggled to understand how to begin investing, or you want to know that you're on the right track, this is an essential read.

The second book, **Get Smart or Get Screwed: How To Select The Best and Get The Most From Your Financial Advisor**(originally titled, "Why I Don't Trust Stockbrokers and You Shouldn't Either") provides an overview of the various types of financial brokers and advisors and the services they can (and should) offer. Paul offers compelling insights to help you make the best choices for get the most from whomever you work with; to save you time, grow your money, and give you peace of mind all along the way. Whether you are a first-time or savvy investor, you will learn new ways to avoid the plethora of pitfalls many investors encounter.

The **"How To Invest"** series books are available in paperback and eBook formats and can be purchased via Amazon and other outlets, or at http://www.PaulMerriman.com.

This third book, **101 Investment Decisions Guaranteed To Change Your Financial Future**, is the workbook for savvy investors at all stages of life! Learn how every investment decision you make has the potential to add $1,000 or more to your wealth. Together, this can mean millions of extra dollars for you and your family over the years. In his straightforward, pull-no-punches style, Paul Merriman explains the decisions to be made and the impact of each on your financial future, making it easy to prioritize and make the best financial choices for your goals.

For articles, podcasts, updated mutual fund recommendations and more, visit: http://www.PaulMerriman.com

Made in the USA
Lexington, KY
15 January 2014